INTERNATIONAL HIGHER EDUCATION SYSTEMS

New Edition

JOHN P. EDDY
STANLEY D. MURPHY

University Press of America, Inc.
Lanham • New York • Oxford

Copyright © 2000 by
University Press of America
4720 Boston Way
Lanham, Maryland 20706

12 Hid's Copse Rd.
Cumnor Hill, Oxford OX2 9JJ

Eddy, John.
International higher education systems / John P. Eddy, Stanley D. Murphy.—
New ed.
p. cm.
Includes bibliographical references.
1. Education, Higher—Cross-cultural studies. 2. Higher education and state—
Cross-cultural studies. 3. International education. I. Murphy, Stanley D. II.
Title
LB2322.2.E33   2000   378—dc21   00-041173 CIP

ISBN 0-7618-1748-4 (pbk: alk. ppr.)

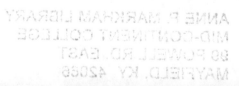

Contents

Foreword

As global educators working in institutions of higher education, the crucial question to be addressed is, "what should we do to create policies and programs that are effective and sensitive to the many issues that tend to divide us or bring us together in colleges and universities—as well as society—in our global village? This book attempts to take an ethnographic, knowledge based on descriptive anthropology, and phenomenological, knowledge based on phenomena approach to assist the reader on how to assess international situations to determine possible decision making opportunities in higher education. This position is drawn from a wide range of research studies and observations.

This reference work looks at several perspectives by determining higher education situations in nations as positive or negative factors for development and progress. These key factors include:

1. Events such as violence and wars, acts of God, and economic and political reactions;
2. Cultural issues;
3. Governmental policies and programs or lack of policies and programs as well as their enforcement or lack of enforcement; and
4. Resources available for higher education development and progress.

What can students of higher education gain from this reference book? Some selective benefits are:

1. An understanding and appreciation of the complexity of international higher education decision making involving the previously mentioned factors;

2. A knowledge of American higher education compared to other select nations and how this knowledge can employ educated persons abroad; and
3. A basic overview of selected higher education institutions overseas and their outstanding characteristics as world class leaders.

To illustrate the approach of this book, here is an example of some higher education situations involving various nations.

Situation	Problem	Results
Texas A & M University started a branch campus in Japan	Japanese governmental policies were negative and could not be changed; Cultural expectations of Japanese students were in conflict; Changing economic conditions in the U.S.A. and Japan negated success	The branch campus was closed in August 1994 with a loss of $7 million.
Gang wars in American cities and tribal wars in Africa and Asia	Key factors include cultural conflicts, economic and political reactions, governmental policies and programs; and lack of resources	There is a destructive pattern that continues to take lives and property. This discourages the development of higher education.

Preface and Acknowledgments

The lead author wants to thank his wife, mother, mother-in-law, daughter-in-law, son–in-law, children and grandchildren for their contributions to this book.   Believe it or not, my relatives have helped me think about subjects in this book.

Again, we want to thank colleagues and students for their ideas that have contributed to materials in this book. We appreciate their comments. A special thanks to Jennifer Rimmer for her assistance in the final proof reading of this text.

Moreover, specific colleagues are listed as coauthors in this reference work. We especially thank them for their contributions such as over 200 references from around the world.

Some future journal published articles will have selected material from this book.   Therefore, We thank the following editors for their permission to publish these materials:

1. Dr. George E. Uhlig, Editor of the *College Student Journal,* and
2. Dr. Sulya Nath Prasad, Editor of the *Peace Progress Journal* and the *Peace Education Journal*

There is a trend in shifting the focus on international programs in 1994 due to a number of changing world conditions from the U.S.A. to nations overseas (Heginbotham, 1994, October 19).   Some of these changing conditions are:

1. The financial constraints and shortcomings of higher education institutions in the U.S.A. have caused many colleges and universities to cut international programs abroad.

2. The ending of the Cold War and the fall of Communism worldwide has caused a need for different kinds of international programs moving from the traditional area of study to "problem-focused programs" (Heginbotham, 1994, October 19).

These "problem-focused programs" include such subjects as:

1. How to develop democratic type government with workable and responsive two party electoral systems, parliamentary governing bodies, local governments and multiparty political parties.
2. How to develop independent and professional media.
3. How to develop and institutionalize the rule of law, human rights, legal due process and procedures within courts for an independent judiciary.
4. How to develop independent and accountable educational institutions.
5. How to develop and improve environmental policies to wisely use natural resources for the present and future needs.
6. How to revise traditional international programs to better serve problem-oriented needs in different countries.

International education means we are in the global village as neighbors (Eddy and Associates, 1985). It is important that leaders in government, foundations and higher education across the world will respond to the complex new international realities (Heginbotham, 1994, October 19). There is an essential need for those involved in international education to make necessary changes to meet these new needs if this vital area is to be better served.

References

Eddy, J.P. and Associates, (1985). *International education and student development applications.* Minneapolis, Minnesota: Alpha Editions of Burgess International Publishers.

Heginbotham, S. J. (1994, October 19). Shifting the focus of international programs. *The Chronicle of Higher Education.* Page A68.

Chapter 1

ഇ൰ഌ

Introduction to the New Edition of
International Higher Education Systems

JOHN P. EDDY AND STANLEY D. MURPHY

The new edition of *International Higher Education Systems* has one new author, Stanley D. Murphy, Interim Director of Counseling at Austin Peay State University. Murphy has co-authored two books, published numerous national refereed professional articles and held responsible positions of leadership in several universities as an administrator, professor and clergyman. He recently completed the Education Specialist (Ed.S.) Degree in Administration and Supervision from Middle Tennessee State University and plans to complete his doctorate (Ed.D.) at Tennessee State University in Higher Education Administration.

This is the second edition of this book. This means the book was good enough to go into a second edition. The first edition was well received and evaluated by numerous students as well as professionals in the field of international education. This second edition includes new material and research useful to those who work with international students, international academic programs around the world, and international business relations overseas. Some of the same information given in the first edition is repeated here because it is important and valuable to the reader who wants to understand other countries, cultures and their educational systems.

There is a tendency among some American higher education personnel to discount the values of higher education in other lands. This elitist approach is damaging and dangerous to higher education. Believing nothing can be learned from other nations is damaging in limiting knowledge and dangerous in building bias.

At the end of each chapter are references for the readers to delve more deeply into the subject matter covered. Readers are encouraged to read other books, journals, reports and materials on higher education institutions worldwide to obtain a more comprehensive and complete picture beyond this reference work.

Another helpful feature of this book is the key reference list which includes valuable books and articles that can be used for research on higher education institutions world-wide. This reference list represents books and articles published in this country and overseas.

The following table introduces contemporary representative problems around the world facing higher education.

Table 1.1
KEEPING TRACK
FROM TOP OF THE CLASS TO THE BOTTOM

Comparing the United States with nine other selected countries

In the 1950's the U.S. high school graduation rate was among the highest in the developed world.	But in the 1980's other countries moved into the top rank . . .	. . . and now the U.S. is falling behind.

Approximate percentage earning a diploma:

%	1950's	%	1980's	%	now
		100%	Czech Republic, Norway –	100%	Finland, Norway, Poland, South Korea –
90		90	Canada, Finland –	90	
80	Czech Republic, Germany, **United States**	80	Germany, Poland, South –	80	Czech Republic –
70	Norway	70	Korea, **United States** –	70	France, Germany
60		60		60	
50	Canada, Finland, Poland	50	France –	50	Canada, Ireland,
40	France, Ireland	40		40	**United States**
30		30	Ireland –	30	
20	South Korea	20		20	
10		10		10	
0		0		0	

Source: "Education at a Glance: OECD Indicators 1998", Organization for Economic cooperation and Development

Table 1.2
Questions To Ask of Higher Education Worldwide

Are These Questions Repeating Themselves In Other Countries?

	Questions to Ask	Reason for Answer
1	Why have ten elite universities in **England** decided to unite together in 1994?	With a severe shortage of funds for higher education, they want to preserve money for research or little funds would be available.
2	Why have all institutions of higher education in **Rwanda** been closed in 1994?	Two tribes have been at war fighting and over a million Rwandans have been killed.
3	Why did Texas A & M University close its branch campus in Tokyo, **Japan** in 1994?	The Japanese government failed to accredit the college in Japan so American students couldn't get visas to come into the country and Japanese students didn't favor a nonaccredited institution. Thus, Texas A & M University lost $7,000,000.
4	Why are **Russian** scientists looking for employment in other countries in 1994?	There is little or no money for nuclear work since the breakup of the USSR in 1991.
5	Why are mainland **Chinese** universities suffering from cigarette smoke in their buildings in 1994?	The Chinese government has no campaign against tobacco smoking even though it is the number one killer of its people.
6	Why is **Germany** having difficulties with universities within its eastern area in 1994?	The demise of communism and the reunification of Germany finds the eastern area, that had Marxist oriented professors being replaced, in the ideological shift.
7	Why have the **French** students protested in 1994?	They did not favor the government cutting their scholarship monies.
8	Why have some **Nigerian** universities been closed in 1994?	Strikes have resulted because of faculty protesting low pay for their teaching.

International Experiences that Brought New Insights on Cultures

DR. JOHN PAUL EDDY

The following international experiences brought new insights to me:

1. In 1954, I traveled to the Philippines to work on a medical, agricultural, and educational program in Kidapawan, Cotabato, and Mindanao. The multicultural insights of this experience were outstanding as I also studied in a local college, worked at that college and involved students in useful community work projects.

2. In 1970, I traveled to over 20 countries and territories around the world on a United Nations International Education Year Program sponsored by Phi Delta Kappa Educational Fraternity and Bowling Green State University, Bowling Green , Ohio. The opportunity to visit educational institutions and the ministers of education in these nations was incredible.

3. In 1974, I traveled to six European nations and delivered lectures at the Academy of Sciences at the University of Bucharest, Bucharest, Romania at a United Nations sponsored international conference. The trips offered exceptional opportunities to study culture in France, England, Romania, Yugoslavia, Italy and Spain.

4. In 1977, I traveled to Mexico to speak at an International Communications Conference at the University of Monterrey, Monterrey, Mexico. Again I received valuable knowledge from the Mexicans and from scholars around the world at this conference.

5. In 1978, I traveled to Canada to speak at an International Higher Education Conference at the University of Calgary, Calgary, Canada. This proved to be helpful in studying Native Americans in North America.

6. In 1985, I traveled to Mexico as a guest of U.S. Navy Seminar in San Diego, California. I was able to visit valuable museums to study Mexican and Native Indian Culture.

7. In 1987, I traveled to Mexico's Copper Canyon with faculty and students from Texas sponsored by Temple Junior College, Temple, Texas. I gave a lecture during the science seminar and was able to study Mexican culture via museums.

8. In 1992, I traveled and gave lectures at King Saud University, Riyadh in Saudi Arabia and at the University of Guam in Agana, Guam. The opportunity presented me a chance to study the cultures of the Middle East Region and the South Pacific Region.

9. In 1994, I traveled to Alaska—flying over parts of Canada—to give a lecture at the University of Alaska at Fairbanks, Fairbanks, Alaska. While in the area, I visited numerous museums to study Eskimo and Native American cultures. It was also interesting to observe the influence of Russian settlers on the culture of Alaska.

Questions to Ask of Students Who Have been Abroad: A Self Interview

1. What countries have you visited?
2. Have you studied at any school or college abroad—if so, at what institutions?
3. What courses did you study overseas?
4. Have you used Internet Computer Systems to communicate with persons overseas? If so, what countries have you reached?
5. Do you communicate regularly by mail with persons in other countries?
6. Do you make phone calls regularly to persons in other nations?
7. Do you regularly read books published in other countries?
8. Do you regularly read books about other nations?
9. Would you take a job in another country if the terms and conditions were comparable to those found in the U.S.A.?
10. Would you study in another nation if you had a scholarship offered to you?
11. If you have traveled or studied abroad, what new insights did you obtain?
12. What do you believe higher education institutions in all countries should be doing about international education worldwide?

Does Study Abroad Make A Difference?

Over the years, this question is often raised: Does study abroad make a difference? The obvious answer given is that it does bring values to the student throughout one's life. Many examples of these values might be provided through the lives of former students who studied overseas. For example, Dr. Anna Robertson Brown (1893) studied at Oxford University in England and College de France in France. She went on to write over 34 books including the best-seller book entitled, *What Is Worthwhile?* This book went into 73 printings for 67 years and was translated into Japanese (Campion, 1994).

Dr. Brown asks a number of questions, of every reader of her book, about what is important in life such as:

1. "What is worthwhile?"
2. "What is vital?"
3. "What may we profitably let go?"

Some of the valuable ideas of Dr. Brown (1893) in this book includes four things to avoid encumbering over lives with such as: (1) Drop pretense; (2) Drop worry; (3) Let go of discontent; and (4) Let go of self-seeking. Again, Dr. Brown suggests eight values that can improve our lives such as: (1) Value the use of time; (2) Value work by questioning if it is character building and helping others; (3) Value seeking daily happiness; (4) Value cherishing love; (5) Value keeping ambition in check; (6) Value developing friendships; (7) Value not fearing sorrow as disappointments are inevitable; and (8) Value faith in God so to face the constant challenges of life.

It is difficult to add to the lists that Dr. Brown has so wisely put together from her study abroad and writing of 34 books to support her thesis of what is worthwhile in life. However, I would add two more values to Dr. Brown's list of eight to include: (9) Value never giving up on important things in life; and (10) Value traveling abroad to discover new ideas, new experiences and new cultures.

I would illustrate these two values, just mentioned, by referring to an article I recently read about a former English military officer who was in Burma in World War II as a prisoner of war of the Japanese at the River Kwai. The prisoner of war camp there is the theme of a famous book and movie on this experience. Eric Lomax from Edinburgh, Scotland, was severely beaten while in the camp and his beating was witnessed by Takashi Nagase, a Japanese army interpreter (Ehrlich, 1994). Years later, Mr. Nagase wrote a book entitled *Crosses and Tigers* in which Mr. Lomax's terrible torture was described (Nagase, 1986). Finally the two men got together on March 26, 1993 in Kanchanaburi, Burma at the site of the World War II museum near the River Kwai, nearly 50 years since their first encounter.

This story illustrates how two men from different cultures never gave up trying to overcome those horrible experiences at the River Kwai Prisoner of War Camp during World War II. Their reconciliation, after nearly half a century, provides one of the most memorable true stories of all time of two former war enemies.

These two true stories, about these persons who traveled abroad, provide insight on how "sensitive souls" can gain much from their overseas adventures. A number of years ago, I met the author of the book, *The Ugly American*, which tells tales of insensitive Americans traveling abroad. This book demonstrates my point that one has to be sensitive to persons in order to gain valuable insights abroad such as seen here in the lives of Anna Robertson Brown, Eric Lomax and Tokashi Nagase.

In understanding international higher education systems in the professoriate in higher education abroad (Boyer, Altbach and Whitelow, 1994), it is also important to have some guidelines for sensitivity to what is worthwhile in life. This chapter has provided such guidelines for those who would study personnel and programs in higher education across the world. For example, the Japanese recognized the importance of Brown's book, *What Is Worthwhile?,* and translated it into Japanese. Again, a Japanese author Nagase wrote a book, *Crosses and Tigers,* that helped two former enemies become friends. The moral of this message is that as persons around the world become involved in the literature and experiences in other nations, persons develop improved attitudes and actions towards one another.

As one studies conditions of countries across the world, many observations can be made that reveal how nations can be affected by situations in these nations. It is estimated in the U.S.A. that the cost of liability suits, higher insurance rates, defensive medicine and so forth is about $400 billion or about 10 percent of total national output. For example, with 5 percent of the world's population, the U.S.A. uses 30 percent of the world's resources and it has 70 percent of the world's lawyers. Excessive legislation in the U.S.A. continues to hurt economic growth endowments. In Japan, there is one lawyer for every 10 engineers but in the U.S.A. there are 500 lawyers for every 10 engineers. The question is raised as to which nation might be expected to grow faster— Japan or the U.S.A.? (Stratagem, 1994).

Japan has the second strongest economy in the world next to the United States with 126 million people. For example, international trade with Japan and other countries is evident in Denton, Texas with Sally Beauty Supply Company—a $630 million company whose headquarters have been in Denton since 1982. This company has stores in England, Scotland, Northern Ireland, Puerto Rico and Japan. In 1987, Sally Beauty Supply became the only international beauty supply company when it purchased the largest beauty supply organization in the United Kingdom.

Two New Key Books On International Higher Education

Two new key books on international higher education are:

1. Wickremasinghe, W. (1992). *Handbook of world education.* Houston, Texas: American collegiate Service. (A book covering elementary, secondary and higher education in over 100 countries of the world.)
2. Boyer, E.L., Altbach, P.G., and Whitelow, M.J. (1994). *The academic profession: An international perspective.* Princeton, New Jersey: The Carnegie Foundation for the Advancement of Teaching. (A book that is one of the first known studies of professors in fourteen countries of the world and their views on higher education subjects.)

The importance of these books to present the concepts of global interdependence and the need to understand the global era of cooperation and understanding among nations cannot be underestimated. These books provide valuable reference material for both the academic community and those businesses and agencies that have an interest in international education.

These two books together present some of the finest current materials on higher education published up to this time. The weaknesses of both books is that neither present specific higher education research studies in various nations of the world such as is presented in this reference book from Nigeria to Saudi Arabia. Thus, these three books together present some of the most current international higher education material.

The Handbook of Education provides some of the latest and most authoritative information on the systems of higher education around the world in over 100 countries all in one volume of nearly 1,000 pages. A comparative book is the *International Encyclopedia of Education* that comes in over 12 volumes, published by Husen and Postlethwaite of New York City.

The Academic Profession covers a study of professors in 14 different countries. Some of the main findings from this book include the following:

1. The professoriate average age is between 40 and 50 years with the majority men.

2. The view of the professoriate on high school graduates that should go to college range from Russia at 30 percent to Germany at 73 percent.

3. The view of the professoriate on their academic discipline finds a majority rating it very important to them. Pressure to publish does not reduce the quality of teaching according to professors in 13 of the 14 nations.

4. The opinion of the professoriate on working conditions is that in 12 of the 14 countries the professors feel that they are underpaid. Only in Hong Kong, soon to be under the rule of China, and in the Netherlands do faculty rate their salaries as good or excellent.

5. The problem of university governance is that in most countries the professoriate feel alienated with the highest administrators with Japan and Korea being the most content. In 6 of the 14 countries, a lack of faculty involvement is a problem. Only in Japan, do the majority of the professors claim their top administrators are providing excellent leadership.

6. When asked of how much government should define the overall policies of higher education, the professors affirmative responses ranged from 90 percent in Russia to 10 percent in the United States. With regard to too much interference by the government, the highest was Korea with 90 percent and the lowest was Chile with 17 percent.

7. With regard to internationalizing higher education, professors say the highest is Japan with 81 percent and the lowest is Korea with 12 percent of their students studying in other countries.

8. Looking at the future of higher education, three issues are apparent that professors identify as most important. They are as follows:

    a) Student access should be made available to all who can meet the standards of admission.
    b) Governance, using the "industrial model," has caused a breakdown of collegiality resulting in many faculty feeling that they have lost control of their institutional decision making processes.
    c) The continued tension between teaching, research, publishing and service causes faculty problems. Teaching is not given the status or credit that it ought to receive.

There is a growing network of scholars across the world who are communicating and consulting with each other. The Internet computer network is assisting the exchange of knowledge between faculty in different nations. These connections between the professoriate are developing daily and these associations will strengthen the opportunities for improving higher education worldwide as we live in the global village.

Comparing United States And European College Education

First, in the United States if you are a college educated person don't avoid manual labor. In fact, some United States colleges encourage their students to do manual labor in jobs at the colleges. Winston S. Churchill, grandson of the famous prime Minister of England, tells of visiting Dr. Albert Schweitzer, when he was 88 years old, in Lambarene, Gabon, Africa. Schweitzer had four doctoral degrees—one in theology, one in philosophy, one in music and one in medicine. He spent over 50 years as a medical missionary serving without salary to thousands of Africans. One day, Schweitzer cut a tree down in the rain forest of Equatorial Africa. He needed help to turn the tree over. An African, educated in England, stood nearby in a smart suit. Schweitzer asked his aid with the tree. The man said, "You misunderstand, I am an educated person—I don't do manual labor!" Schweitzer commented that this state of mind is not only held by some in Africa but in Britain and other European countries by those who received university education and feel the world owes them a living [Churchhill, W.S. (1989). *Memories and adventures*. New York:

Weidenfeld and Nicholson, pl. 153]. Alexander Wollcott, once spoke of the great virtue of work, and said, "I admire work like everything, I can sit and watch it by the hour." [Shoemaker, S. (1965). *Extraordinary living for ordinary men.* Grand Rapids, Michigan: Zondervan Publishing House, p. 29]

Second, after having students from 26 different nations of the world study with me, I have asked them why are you getting your college and university degrees in America? The overwhelming answer has been, "Because in America you teach more than theories and your courses have practical applications to the world of work." Again, foreign students have told me that in America there are several other important values in higher education such as:

1. There are more choices for academic and professional fields to study.
2. The equipment in these disciplines is more modern and up-to-date.
3. The professors are more friendly and helpful.
4. There are more jobs available on campus and in nearby cities for employment at a higher wage.
5. When you graduate from an American college the degree is often worth more than a degree from their country.
6. The resources of American institutions of higher education from libraries to laboratories and from books to computers far excels what they have in their nations.
7. American colleges have valuable student services to help develop students in their extracurricular activities.
8. Foreign student host families have helped some students discover the hospitality and cordiality of American families.

Of course, American higher education is far from perfect. American society also has its shortcomings as we try to eliminate racism, sexism, and other prejudices against peoples. This nation is struggling with violence everywhere and many persons get killed or crippled by guns, drugs and abuse. It is a shock to many international students to see the violence in America in our films and sometimes in our streets. We have a long way to go to make our country a safer and more caring community.

Why Foreign Students Study in the United States and Not in Their Home Country

Recently, I asked a doctoral student from India why she was studying for her doctorate in Higher Education Administration in the USA and not India or England. Her answer was that in both India and England graduate work is done individually with one mentor professor. One does not take courses on special subjects but does mostly literature searches in libraries in developing one's papers and dissertation. Therefore, the graduate student misses out on covering specific subject matter credit courses by a number of expert professors teaching these classes. Thus, the Higher Education Administration doctoral program in the USA is much preferred by her.

Philosophy and Practices to World Higher Education

There is a need to develop a philosophy for world higher education to reveal some needed standards across the earth for college and university leaders to develop their institutions into models for knowledge, activities, research, service, pedagogy, and concern for the best welfare of persons. Oliver Stone's 1994 film "Natural Born Killers" is a sad commentary on the American film industry. The film highlights America's obsession with violence. College graduates in America should have models that teach solid proven life values. Some of these models are shared here for the development and implementation of standards in all higher education institutions worldwide.

Table 1.3

Proposed Standards	Existing Models
Multicultural human rights and freedom principles for possible policies in all higher education institutions.	United Nations Document for Human Rights (Coauthored by U.S. Ambassador Eleanor Roosevelt).
College student philosophy and principles for guidelines dealing with persons in higher education [In book, Eddy, J.P. (1977). College Student Personnel Development. Administration and Counseling. Washington, D.C.: University Press of America.]	U.S.A. Student Point of View of American Council of Education 1939 and 1941 (authors such as Gilbert Wrenn and Dr. E. G. Williamson)
Environmental standards for preserving and protecting our air, water, land, animals, plants and life on earth.	North American Agreement on Environmental Cooperation, 1993 signed by leaders from U.S.A., Canada, and Mexico
College student services standards for dealing with students and staff in colleges and universities.	Standards for higher education: Bryan, W. A.; Winston, R. B.; and Miller, T. K. (1991). Using professional standards in student affairs. San Francisco, California: Jossey-Bass, Inc., Publishers.
Prevention of human conflicts and wars on this planet through: peace education taught in schools and colleges; United Nations peace helping efforts; volunteer organizations that provide food, clothing, shelter, water wells, agricultural education for self-help and positive mental health motivation materials.	A) International Association of Educators for World Peace documents and annual journals, Peace Progress Journal and Peace Education Journal both published in India. B) Self help volunteer organization directories worldwide.
Drug free and healthy living practices covering the most healthy foods, the best exercise methods, the proven relaxation approaches, the known stress reduction modes and other helpful life style strategies for useful physical, mental, emotional, intellectual, social and spiritual health.	Higher education student health centers at major U.S.A. universities where a wellness and holistic philosophy of health prevention, intervention and treatment is provided in theories and practices.
Ethical and professional practices in higher education for teaching, counseling, advising and relating with persons.	The current professional and ethical statements of the American College Personnel Association, American Counseling Association, the National Association of Student Personnel Administrators and the American Psychological Association.

References

Boyer, E. L., Altbach, P.G. and Whitelow, M. J. (1994). *The academic profession: An international perspective.* Princeton, New Jersey: The Carnegie Foundation for the Advancement of Teaching.

Brown, A. R. (1893). *What is worthwhile?* New York, New York: Thomas Y. Crowell Publisher.

Campion, N. R. (1994, July). What really is worthwhile. *Reader's Digest,* 130-132.

Ehrlich, P. (1994, October). Eric Lomax's long journey. *Reader's Digest,* 99-106.

Lederer, W. J. (1958). *The Ugly American.* New York, New York: Norton Publishers.

Nagase, T. (1986). *Crosses and Tigers.* Tokyo, Japan: Iwanami Shoten Publishers.

Wickremasinghe, W. (1992). *Handbook of world education.* Houston, Texas: American Collegiate Service.

———(1994), September-October. Global investing for long-term performance. *Stratagem,* 2.

Chapter 2

ଗଔ

Addressing Issues in Higher Education in America and Worldwide

Closing Colleges and Universities Worldwide

How sad it is to hear when a nation's higher education institutions are closed for months and even years due to a strike or a war. Some of my graduate students from Nigeria and Lebanon know of what I am saying here for they have experienced this terrible condition of not being able to teach or learn. Educating leaders to mediate effectively to avoid strikes and wars is an essential investment for peace, productivity, progress and prosperity.

Violence in our World is Destroying Us

We need a required course in all our schools and colleges titled "violence prevention education" which teaches children and adults to avoid using the violence of words and of abuse against persons. In these courses, content should address how to be a positive, accepting person, how to be a constructive parent, how to mediate conflicts to prevent violence, how to provide a witness to develop wholesome persons, and how to identify the dangers of weapons, drugs and abuse. The need is evident from Rwanda, Africa to Nazi Germany to Los Angeles, California.

Scholarship Sports and Higher Education

Some American higher education institutions shamefully spend more money per student on their athletic scholarship sports program than they do in providing scholarships for their needy students. The lack of adequate financial aid in some colleges is a disgrace to our human race.

Ethics and Higher Education

Every higher education curricular area should have a unit or even a course on ethics because many college graduates shamelessly ruin their careers with dishonest behavior from college presidents to corporate lawyers.

Military Veterans and Higher Education

It is amazing how America can send its military men and women into wars and when these service personnel return to get a college degree, our government will not provide for adequate higher education needs.

Corporate Makeover and Takeover of Higher Education

The tragedy of contemporary America is that many higher education institutions are copying and using cosmetic restructuring similar to that of corporate America is doing by paying their high executives outrageous salaries and benefits. The gap between faculty salaries is a negative morale factor destroying the collegiate community. Using phony market value strategies, administrators argue to pad their pocketbooks.

Demanding More of College Students

There is need to demand more not less of college students in academic work if they are to develop holistically—body, mind and spirit. One cannot grow if not challenged to set goals and to work to meet goals.

Learning to Work Together in Higher Education

Learning to work together is the greatest need in higher education where persons tend to be competitive rather than cooperative and individualistic rather than collectivistic in behavior. The self-directed work team or "directed dyad" is the answer to learning how to set goals, to motivate goals and to reach goals as partners in the process for progress.

Recognizing What an Education Really Means

Unfortunately, across the world college students are graduating with a university degree and inability to function in the real world due to self defeating philosophies such as:

1. An inability to do manual labor because the university graduate is not to do such things and
2. An inability to work with uneducated persons because such persons are not worth the time or a university graduate.

Faculty Give Away Governance

A serious problem of faculty at some colleges and universities is that some of the faculty let administrators make all the decisions and in turn blame administrators for being dictators, manipulators and traitors against higher education.

Lack of College Student Input

It is strange how, over the years, some American colleges have allowed college students to give their ideas to improve their institution while other universities have not once used the talents of their students' creative minds on committees.

Democracy Lost for 188 Years

How could America wait 188 years from 1776 (Declaration of Independence) to 1964 (Civil Rights Act) before all Americans were eligible to get their voting rights?

Research Oriented Teaching

There is a desperate need for research oriented teaching whereby professors provide research evidence for their assumptions on higher education. From research on college student development to research on common themes of state higher education coordinating boards, information needs to be presented in our graduate courses so we have current and relevant knowledge. For example, Nwafor and Eddy (1993) identifies twenty different areas in which college students have developed using the "directed dyad" method of Eddy.

American Indian Tribes as Nations

The American Indian tribes, sometimes recognized as sovereign nations, have been a part of our nation's history. Unfortunately, our government has broken treaty after treaty with native Americans beginning in 1776 when our nation was born after breaking off from its colony status within England. Even President John Kennedy, who campaigned in 1960 to get Native American votes, betrayed the New York Mohawk tribe when he rejected a treaty signed by President George Washington to allow a dam to be built over the best of its lands to destroy its agricultural and cultural heritage forever. Native Americans have had to fight for their lands and their rights in the courts. More of these lawsuits have been won to gain back their territories and their freedom.

Alcohol and Medicine Disasters

The chemical reactions in the abuse of alcohol and mixing of some chemicals worldwide has meant death and the destruction of body organs such as the liver. Some examples are:

1. Beer or alcoholic drinks and barbiturates;
2. Wine or alcoholic drinks and Tylenol, and
3. Whisky or alcoholic drinks and Valium.

These are but a few of the more common dangerous combinations that have killed or crippled children, youth and adults. The authors have known of such deaths and permanent body organ damage in college settings. A "wisdom seminar" is needed in our schools and colleges to warn that alcohol alone can be dangerous but even more dangerous when mixed with certain medicines. Again, people need to be warned about alcoholic poisoning which occurs when large amounts of alcohol are consumed. Youth who challenge each other to games or contests to see who can drink the most alcohol have been known to die even at colleges in 1994. Higher education should take stronger leadership in alcohol, tobacco and other drug education.

Life Is A Fragile Thing

The lead author lives in that northeast part of Texas where the farmers often lose crops as follows: (1) the sun burns up the crop; (2) the floods drown the crop; (3) the drought dries up the crop.   There is a moral lesson here in life such as too much of anything can kill. Living in this environment keeps one aware of how fragile life is for all of us. Those who make their living in agriculture worldwide face these cruel elements so these farmers face fragile futility. The author recalls a similar climate in the Philippines where he worked years ago and how it taught him great truths of life not found in books. Perhaps the most practical philosophers of survival of the world are not the university professors of philosophy but the fragile farmers described here. This is recorded here to give perspective to faculty and administrators of higher education institutions who may look down on uneducated or even illiterate farmers or others on our planet. Degrees from universities do not necessarily make persons of wisdom, kindness or of concern for others.

When Communism and Fascism Collapses

When non-democratic governments such as communist or fascist governments collapse, what happens? The results are seen in Eastern Europe and Central America. It is a miracle to have freedom for these peoples and to see democracy develop. However, the transitions from authoritarian government to democratic government are very hard. Thus, nations changing from dictatorships to democracies often suffer from inflation, unemployment, food shortages and other problems. Higher education institutions could help in this effort with self-help classes on television. It is important for other established democratic nations to come to the rescue of these former authoritarian governments with food and financial aid as well as educators to help train persons to be independent capitalists and small business persons. From training persons to raise their own food with city and country gardens, fish ponds and bird feeders to teaching persons how to make their own clothes and ride bikes for transportation, this can make persons independent. *Habitats for Humanity* can teach persons to make their own homes, with volunteers, so persons can move out of unsafe apartment complexes or huts.

Restructuring: Pros and Cons

Restructuring* is the "in word" in American higher education as our colleges and universities copy what has been happening in the corporations around the world. The purposes leaders give for restructuring are to revitalize or reorganize departments, downsize staffing, save costs, and increase productivity. For the past two years, the authors have interviewed faculty from coast to coast and border to border on restructuring results. The evidence is presented here in advantages and disadvantages. Research did not include Texas colleges.

Advantages of restructuring seem to be: (1) Some faculty are working together; (2) Some faculty have better offices and technological equipment; (3) Some faculty have more travel money and grants funding; and (4) Some faculty are recognized more in newsletters.

Disadvantages of restructuring seem to be: (1) The promised cost savings have been lost and gone into more assistant deans who have more secretaries; (2) Some faculty feel they are treated more impersonally and have greater problems in doing their work than before; (3) Some faculty have retired, gone on leave or taken positions elsewhere to avoid the effects of restructuring; (4) Some faculty feel there are, more than ever before, special interest groups created that divide them further as faculty; (5) The restructuring has provided many faculty with less phone money, duplication money and control over the technology in their area from duplication machines and computers to phones; (6) The restructuring has caused many secretaries to leave or transfer so that the new replacements cause additional faculty problems from mistakes to inexperience; (7) The restructuring has also meant for faculty: heavier teaching and student advising loads; longer waiting periods to duplicate teaching materials; and more secretarial type scheduling of their students from exams to dissertations; (8) Some faculty have also been angry over: their offices being relocated, their salaries being less, their secretaries being moved and their students having difficulty finding their academic area. As a result, some faculty have sued their leader because of less favored treatment than other faculty.

---

* *The term re-engineering is also the code word used along with the methods called, "process redesign." Some of this goes with W. Edwards Deming's approach which is covered in Appendix B of this book along with a reference list of books to be used with this approach.*

In summary, this was not a scientific study but only clinical observations from interviews and conversations with professors from a dozen different public universities around the nation. The results, perhaps, reflect more the problems of changing environment once the restructuring takes place than any single finding from faculty comments. In conclusion, some faculty like the restructuring and others dislike the results which is what happens in any changing situation. Again, the observations here are not meant to be taken as representative of any one institution of higher education or groups of institutions that have gone through restructuring.

Saving Money When Restructuring on Phone Bills

1. Share a phone with another colleague to cut expenses.
2. Discover toll free numbers (1-800) and use them.
3. Ask students to call you at home at night after 10:00 p.m. so you don't play "phone tag" trying to reach them.
4. When you return a long distance call, tell the person who called you to call you back as your phone budget doesn't allow for sufficient communication time.
5. Make long distance calls at your home to students and colleagues across the country to reduce your university phone costs.
6. Check your university phone bill for possible mistakes every month.
7. Write letters to your students, far from the university, to tell them to call you at night after 10:00 p.m.
8. If you are a state or national officer of a professional organization, try to get them to provide you with phone money to reimburse your university phone account.
9. Ask colleagues to share professional long distance calls by taking turns.
10. *Refuse to make some calls that are long distance.

---

*　*Use Internet computer systems and save these costly calls.*

Avoiding International Higher Education Institution Mistakes

In August, 1994 Texas A&M University closed its international branch campus in Tokyo, Japan after losing over $7,000,000. How could that serious loss have been avoided? The Japanese government would not accredit the University's program in Japan as this discouraged Japanese students from taking courses there even as it disallowed American students from getting visas to study there. Clearly no foreign college should start a branch campus in any country when the government of that nation will not accredit its programs. When higher education leaders make decisions, they must look at all the barriers from the success of a new project and weigh these carefully before moving ahead. Texas A&M University, along with nineteen other American universities, have closed their campuses in Japan and lost millions of dollars of money that also hurt their programs in the United States of America. This case study illustrates the importance of a doctoral program in higher education administration that deals with such vital studies.

Stopping the Losses In Higher Education Scholarship Athletic Programs

In the state of Texas, two universities in the late 1980s dropped scholarship athletic programs that were costing them annually from hundreds of thousands to millions of dollars. The University of Texas at Arlington dropped its men's football program and Texas Woman's University dropped its women's softball and track programs. These were difficult decisions in a culture that gives so much emphasis to intercollegiate sports. The results at both universities were no losses of student enrollment due to these sports being dropped but a saving of millions of dollars to be used for student academic needs. Often foreign students from countries around the world marvel at the billions of dollar Americans spend on sports compared to what is spent in their countries in colleges and universities. Americans pay a price for their support of intercollegiate athletic scholarships especially in men's football when only about thirty institutions pay their way.

Multicultural Issues in Higher Education Worldwide

Around the world there is evidence of the need for multicultural education for ethnic groups in nation after nation from Rwanda to Bosnia that are fighting each other. Millions of persons are being killed, crippled and displaced to other countries to avoid death. The American model for multicultural education is needed from the Civil Rights Act of 1964 that outlaws discrimination between persons based on race to school and college multicultural education programs that teach tolerance and nonviolence between ethnic persons and groups. The United States has produced some excellent textbooks, videotapes and other materials in multicultural education that needs to be reworded for other countries and translated into other languages.

The High Cost of Drug Abuse For Insurance In Higher Education

There is a higher cost of health insurance for employees at colleges and universities where a significant number are suffering from tobacco, alcohol, and drug abuse problems. These legal drugs for adults cost the lives of over 600,000 in America alone each year. Millions of other diseases, emphysema and other problems are due to these drugs. In China, there are universities where there are no bans on smoking and in 1994 reports from foreign visitors are that conditions are unbearable to breathe in some campus buildings due to smoking. What can be done to reduce these deaths and save billions of dollars because of tobacco and alcohol abuses? The answers are lengthy but the truth is this nation does have excellent stop smoking and cease drinking programs that work. Again, the problem is to get persons into these programs to save their lives, health and the health insurance costs. Higher education institutions need to be more proactive to save the lives of their employees and provide a better environment for all who work at colleges and universities.

Religious Leaders And Higher Education

Some of the most disappointing news in the past five years in America has been the moral fall of prominent preachers who had connections to church colleges. In every case, these church colleges have been badly hurt by these preachers' poor examples. A sick formula for the plague of these preachers has been greed for more power, status, money, admiration, control, and pleasure. We expect religious leaders to be ethical examples. When they are not good role models, it harms the people of the institutions they serve. The life-style of these preachers was unbecoming of their clergy careers. It seems all leaders need to study carefully the case studies of these religious leaders involved with higher education institutions. When leaders desire to put their own personal desires and drives before others, they are in danger of losing their sanity, their families, jobs, careers and reputations. One preacher said, "We lived like kings. We were treated like royalty, showered with generosity, trips and gifts," Sherman, R. [September 29-October 5, 1994) "The last temptation of Joel Gregory," *Dallas Observer,* 604,16-25].

References

Eddy, J. P. (1993), *Higher Education Perspectives for Leaders*. Edina, Minnesota: Burgess International Group Publishing, 93-109.

Nwafor, S. and Eddy, J. P. (1993). Dyad: An Empirical Examination of a Dyad Process to Higher Education Courses. *College Student Journal.* 27(2), 231-233.

Chapter 3

৪০০৪

The Best of Higher Education Around the World

The best of higher education worldwide is what the lead author discovered in visiting over 26 countries of the world from 1932 to 1992 (Eddy, 1993) and by having students from 26 countries of the world study with him from 1954 to 1994. This information provided unusual insights on the best practices observed in countries overseas and what students shared of the best practices they were aware of in their countries.

Higher Education Around the World

The following table introduces the reader to significant discoveries or accomplishments in selected nations worldwide.

Myths of Status in Higher Education Around the World

There are a number of myths about faculty in higher education around the world. As the lead author has visited professors in over 20 nations, he has found the following to be the case: (1) the presence of a window for a professor's office does not measure the professor's productivity in publishing or ability in teaching; (2) the budget for a professor's office

Table 3.1
The Best of Other Countries' Higher Education

Country	Higher Education Institution	Unique Feature
Japan	Tamagawa University Tokyo (private)	Provides some of the best of Western Civilization Studies and Japanese Culture
Italy	Loyola University of Chicago Rome (private)	Provides European History with excellent field trips
Saudi Arabia	King Saud University Riyadh (public)	Provides outstanding petroleum engineering program
Russia	Moscow University Moscow (public)	Provides outstanding aerospace engineering program
England	London University London (public)	Provides good economics program
France	University of Paris Paris (public)	Provides low cost education for foreign students
Thailand	Thailand Public University System	Provides many distance learning courses throughout the nation
Guam, Territory of U.S.A.	University of Guam Agana (public)	Provides outstanding studies on the Pacific region culture
Jamaica	West Indies College (private)	Provides a exemplary model for self-support of the institution and its students
Nigeria	Nigerian Public Higher Education System	Provides manuals for curriculum guides with philosophical assumptions

(continued)

Table 3.1 (continued)
The Best of Other Countries' Higher Education

Country	Higher Education Institution	Unique Feature
Spain	University of Madrid Madrid (public)	Provides an excellent summer program for foreign students visiting the country's cultural highlights
Canada	University of Calgary Calgary, Alberta (public)	Provides college students working in the university union excellent work leadership opportunities
Philippines	Central Mindonao Colleges Kidapawan, Cotabato (private)	Provided a basketball program in 1954 that had a racially integrated team as a world leader
Romania	University of Bucharest Bucharest (public)	Provides valuable higher education studies on Eastern Europe institutions in publications

supplies and equipment does not reflect the accomplishments of a professor in teaching, publishing, advisement or service to an institution.

Creative innovative and productive professors will overcome the institution's inability to give him or her adequate support for his work by personal sacrifice, self-financing and long hours of labor. This is a poor reflection upon the institution, but it is a true observation.

Conclusions on Countries

This chapter has covered a brief approach of selected curricular and extracurricular programs around the world in higher educational institutions. These selections illustrate how colleges and universities in various countries contribute to the progress of higher education.

References

Altback, P. G. (1991). *International higher education: An encyclopedia.* New York, New York: Garland Publishing, Inc.

Altback, P. G.; Kelly, G. P.; and Kelly, D. H. (1981). *International Bibliography of Comparative education.* New York, New York: Praeger.

Altback, P. G. (1980). *University Reform: An international perspective.* Washington, D.C.: AAHE ERIC/Higher Education Research Report Number 10.

Amnesty International Report 1994. (1994). London, England: Amnesty International Publications.

Beck, C. E. (1970). *Perspectives on world education.* New York, New York: William C. Brown.

Boswick, S. (1991). *Guide to universities of Europe.* New York, New York: Facts on File.

Bum, B. B.; Altback, P. G.; Kerr, C.; and Perkins, J. A. (1972). *Higher education in nine countries.* New York, New York: McGraw-Hill Publishers.

Butcher, H. J. and Rudd, E. (1972). *Contemporary problems in higher education.* London, England: McGraw-Hill Publishers.

Commonwealth University Yearbook 1994. London, England: Association of Commonwealth Universities and Longman House.

Eddy, J. P. and Associates. (1985). *International education and student development applications.* Minneapolis, Minnesota: Burgess International Publishers.

Eddy, J. P. (1993). *Higher education perspectives for leaders.* Edina, Minnesota: Burgess International Publishers.

Eddy, J. P. (1977). *College student personnel development, administration and counseling.* Washington, D. C.: University Press of America.

Eicher, J. (1993). Rethinking the finance of post-compulsory education. *International Journal of Educational Research, 19,5.*

El-Khawas, E. (1993). Demographic factors in the staffing of higher education: An international perspective. *Higher Education Management, 5, 127139.*

Goodchild, L. F. and Wechsler, H. S. (1989). *ASHE reader on the history of higher education.* Needhaln Heights, Massachusetts: Ginn Press.

Hoffman, M. S. (1993). *The world almanac and the book of facts 1993.* New York, New York: Pharos Publishers.

Hugill, B. (1994, October 9). University elite in move to break free. *The Observer.* London, England.

Husen, T. and Postlethaite, T. (1985). The international encyclopedia of education: Research and studies. New York, New York: Pergamon Press.

International academic credentials handbook, Volume 1. (1988). *Washington, D. C.: American Association of Collegiate Registrars and Admissions Officers.*

The international encyclopedia of higher education. (1977). San Francisco, California: Jossey-Bass Publishers.

Jessup, G. (1991). *Outcomes: NVO's and the emerging model of education and training.* London, England: The Falmer Press.

Kapur, J. N. (1977). *Current issues in world higher education.* New Delhi, India: Rom Nagar and S. Chand and Company, Ltd.

Kerr, C. (1994). *Higher education cannot escape history.* Albany, New York: State University of New York Press.

Kim, J. E. (1988). *World Education Encyclopedia.* New York, New York: Facts on File Publication.

Kurian, G. T. (1988). *World Education Encyclopedia.* New York, New York: Facts on File Publication.

Mooney, C. J. (1994, June 22). The shared concerns of scholars. *The Chronicle of Higher Education,* A34-38.

UNESCO. (1976). *World guide to education.* Paris, France: Bowker Publishers.

Vanden Bor, J.; Wout, A.; Shute, P.; and James, C. (1991). Higher education in the third world: Status symbols as instruments for development. *Higher Education Journal,* 22(1), 1 15.

Walker, D. (1994). British government puts brakes on growth of university enrollment. *The Chronicle of Higher Education,* 49*.

Wnuk-Lipinska, E. (1990). Polish students after the decline of communism. *European Journal of Education,* 25(4), 400-410.

World guide to higher education: A comparative survey of systems, degrees, and qualifications. (1982). New York, New York: UNESCO, Bowker Publishing Company.

Chapter 4

ℰ○ℭ

Philosophical Tools: How to Develop Thinking of Higher Education Personnel

Philosophical Tools Defined

We all have a bias toward seeking truths, but do we have a system to discover it? Thus, comes this proposal for a comprehensive approach. Philosophical tools defined means certain approaches using the ideas of philosophy to improve the seeking of truth and knowledge for useful decision making in higher education and in all of life's many situations. These philosophical tools for intellectual, moral, physical, emotional, and spiritual decision making are suggested as follows:

1. The scientific truth method is used via Dr. John Dewey of Columbia University to search for human truth;
2. The ethical truth method of Dr. William Perry of Harvard University with Biblical support documentation is used for the moral practice of human behavior;
3. The religious revelation truth method from the Old testament and the New Testament interpreted by the Rev. Billy Graham of Wheaton College, Dr. Maxine Dunham of Asbury

theological Seminary, and the Rev. John Wesley of Oxford University is used for human spiritual and esthetic truths; and

4. The psychological truth method is seen in the behavior of humans toward each other in acts of love, nurture, generosity, faithfulness, and kindness via Dr. Carl Rogers of the University of Chicago and Dr. Howard Clinebell of Claremont Graduate School.

The Media Controls Our Lives By Presenting Its False and Fake Image of the World

What is put on the front page of our newspaper—football scores or hungry person statistics? If more persons knew how many children in America went to bed hungry (emotionally hungry for the love of a parent) and had inadequate food daily, more children might be healthier or even alive today. Even our college newspapers—where supposed educated persons reside—seldom discuss issues of hunger in college towns. It is our values that are wrong. Our values of neglecting the poor, hungry, sick, and unhealthy while supports expensive sports programs of schools and professional athletics.

Ken Starr's FBI Misuse of Justice: A Nazi, KGB and Fascist Approach

The U.S. independent counsel, Ken Starr, recently was questioned on his treatment of Monica Lewinsky. The facts that U.S. President Bill Clinton did break laws are apparent and should be dealt with accordingly, but Mr. Starr also broke laws so he, too, should be dealt with. FBI agents threatened her with 27 years in prison if she didn't talk, denied her legal counsel when she requested it, and kept her for 12 hours o questioning. Then, they tried to get her to put on a tape recorder to entrap the U. S. president in a conversation. These are evil police-state tactics that show how Americans are losing their freedoms, their privacy, and their faith in American justice. For these illegal approaches, Mr. Starr should be fired and reprimanded for illegal witness harassment. His no answer to the Congressmen in his one-day appearance on November 23 concerning these events—as being something he needed to answer later when he knew the answer then—was dishonest and immoral. The philosophy of Mr. Starr is that of the Italian Niccole Machiavelli, who said the end justifies the means no matter how evil the means. Mr. Starr clearly is not a person of justice, but he has taken on the strategies of the evil interrogators of history. *Time* magazine's article by James Carney entitled "The Lone Starr Hearing," November 30, 1998, Pages 39-42, presents some of the evidence of Mr. Starr's testimony. Mr. Starr, like Machiavelli, would use any means, no matter how wicked, to try to get Ms. Lewinsky to obey what he wants to use of her testimony against the U. S president. Mr. Starr shows a dangerous, destructive, and debilitating approach to American justice. It is a retreat to the Salem, Massachusetts, time of the witch trials of 1642 in which all justice was destroyed.

Table 4.1

Issues, Changes, Revisions: Have We Learned From History In American Higher Education?

Issues	Changes	Revision of Changes
Segregation and prejudice against racial groups from 1619 to 1965 — 346 years of history	Affirmative action programs 1965 to 1996 — 31 years	Affirmative action is voted out in California and thrown out in Texas by the fifth Court of Federal Appeals; Texas has passed legislation for opening attendance to public colleges
Federal GI bill for Veterans Act of 1945	Modified to be less for veterans since 1945	Some states have provided additional support for their veterans such as Texas called the Hazelwood Act
A history of governmental leaders who keep reporting scandals of stealing money and harassing their employees	Scandals continue over the years despite policies and penalties	These scandal incidents continue in spite of repeated activity in governmental service given in the mass media coverage and even prison time for persons

Philosophies That Make No Sense: Computer Crisis

On November 28, 1998, I discovered at the world's largest airport—the Fort Worth/Dallas International Airport—the following:

5. that computers run even the toilets at the airport and these toilets do work, but only days ago the computers handling the air control didn't work for nearly 30 minutes to cause dangerous conditions for thousands of airplane passengers who were in planes coming into land and in planes flying out; and

6. that we have computers and great technological equipments, but it sometimes can't operate safely after millions of dollars worth of investments and the computers do better for unnecessary toilet operations than for necessary air control safety operations. What a paradox, what an irony, and what a tragedy of our technological society!

Conclusion

America has tremendous technological computer capacities. However, the priorities of our businesses often are in conflict with a person's safety and security. This true story illustrate the point—toilets before travelers.

Nation of Contradictions:Opposing Philosophies

Who is the U.S. government but whom we elect as our representatives and appoint our leaders and judges to rule our nation?   America is a nation of contradictions in 1998, according to various educational, biological, sociological, philosophical, theological, and political scholars and here is why, seen in Table 4.2:

Table 4.2

Contradiction Item Example	Contrary Position
The U.S. government supports tobacco farmers with money loans and subsidies via its Department of Agriculture in 1998.	The U.S. government's surgeon general and U.S. Department of Education have anti-smoking and anti-tobacco crusades to stop tobacco use.
The U.S. government trains some foreign military in terrorist tactics in schools in America via its Department of Defense in 1998.	Some of these terrorists have been known to kill Americans in nations around the world, so now some Americans oppose the School of the Americas, is but one example.
The U.S. government bombs via its military a country like the Sudan because of suspected terrorist activities in 1998.	The U.S. government allows private U.S. relief organizations to provide aid to the stricken people affected by the bombing losses.
The U.S. government allows certain governmental officials to commit illegal activities in governmental offices while other officials go to jail, pay fines, and are blacklisted for governmental employment in 1998.	The U.S. government has a wide range of law enforcement and justice practices so some persons are caught and punished and others go free without censure.

Why USA Universities Can't Ignore International Issues In 1998 or Any Year

No person who is a student, a faculty member, an administrator, a staff member at an American institution of higher education can neglect the "international factor" in American colleges and universities throughout the nation. From the smallest college to the largest university in America, foreign students attend our institutions to the rate of over 450,000 every year to make America the most popular nation in the world for international students studying in any one nation of the world.

No one can ignore the "international factor" and what its impact is in terms of economic income in America to potential international influence in the years ahead to prevent war and keep the peace between nations with America assuming a strong "peace keeper" role worldwide every year.

For example, how can anyone say that studying about china is not important when one-fourth of the people in the world are from china and at the University of North Texas a number of graduate fields are dominated by Chinese students? How can we ignore Mexico, our neighbor, when it is our biggest trade partner in the world? Colleges and universities depend on relations with nations around the world.

Research and Education for Abstinence as a Lifestyle (REAL): Worldwide International Internet Project

1. Project REAL is available free to persons in more than 200 nations of the world.
2. Project REAL is a private Internet program off campus and a health-issues information system with suggested resources and free 1-800 phone emergency phone numbers.
3. Project REAL is based in Flower Mound, Texas, with a doctoral student at UNT as Web Master.
4. Project REAL's director is Dr. John Paul Eddy, professor of counseling, Development and Higher Education at the University of North Texas.
5. Project REAL deals with health education prevention issues such as: tobacco, alcohol and other drugs; HIV/AIDS; gun control; human violence; peace education; suicide prevention; and other problems.
6. Project REAL keeps up-to-date and new materials are continually added.
7. Project REAL welcomes you to use it daily to help yourself and other persons.
8. Project REAL's Internet code number is www.flash.net/ ~abstain/
9. Project REAL is for children, youth, young persons, adults, senior citizens, educators, business persons, helping professionals, and the general public worldwide.

A Philosophy for Helping Our Teenagers with Health Problems and Preventing College Problems

1. *Teach boys and girls how to say no to sex before marriage.* At United Methodist Church Related University, Emory University, Atlanta, Georgia, a professor found that 84 percent of the teenagers she studied wanted to know how to say no to pre-marital sex.
2. *Teach parents to talk about sexuality* to young children like they do in Denmark. The research results in Denmark show fewer teenage pregnancies, sexual diseases, and HIV/AIDS than in other countries.
3. *Teach boys and girls through programs like True Love Waits*, headquartered in Nashville, Tennessee, supported by many church denominations, which advocates that sexual abstinence before marriage is the best practice.
4. *Teach children to be drug free* because those youth who use drugs tend to get into more pre-marital sex and sexual abuse problems.
5. *Teach our children that in America many businesses use sex* to sell products so that they are not deceived, fooled, or betrayed by false advertising.
6. *Teach children that we care about you, we love you, and we are concerned about you.* That is why we teach you how to handle your sexuality so you have a better life, free from disease, unwanted pregnancy, and bad behavior towards persons.
7. *There is $88 million of federal money* coming to all states on abstinence education, which is abstinence sex education for children in our public schools.
8. *Surveys:* 90 percent of persons believe in sexual education; 85 percent of persons want to include sexual prevention approaches; 12 states only have public school teachers certified to teach sex education.
9. *Good responses to some tough you questions:* This question is a private matter and a confidential matter for me. I'm uncomfortable in answering this question.
10. *Invite outsiders* who are qualified to come in to speak on sexual education.

11. *We need to educate children about the bad choices* and their consequences. Everyone makes mistakes and fails at things, but we still need to try to be morally responsible.

12. *Texas teenagers can now qualify for Medicaid* health care for children who are uninsured and whose families have low incomes. For information on this new plan, call the Texas Department of Human Services at 1-800-252-9330.

Bad Philosophies: Corrupt Leaders in High Places

Pascal, the French philosopher, once wrote: "The heart has its reasons, whereof reason knows nothing."

1. Pope John the 12th in the 9th century was reared by women pilgrims to his St. Peter's Church in the Vatican, and he would take young virgins, youthful women, widows and others who came to Rome. He died in the arms of a prostitute. The treasury of the Roman Catholic Church was drained to support the illegitimate children of Pope John the 12th. The church leadership during his day went into corruption, and its building began to crumble.

2. President John Kennedy was President of the United States from 1960 to 1963, and his extramarital affairs with women were also disgraceful, immoral, adulterous, and sinful but not reported by the media.

3. Kind David is said to have written the book of Psalms and still he committed adultery with Besheba in BC times while her husband was at war.

4. The television evangelists of the 1980's and 1990's, Jimmy Schweiger, James Baker, Robert Tilton, Walker Railey and others, all were in the mass media for their scandalous affairs with women to add to the problem against religion's creditability in those times.

Things We Can Learn from a Dog . . .

1. Never pass up the opportunity to go for a joy ride.
2. Allow the experience of fresh air and the wind in your face to be pure ecstasy.
3. When loved ones come home, always run to greet them.
4. When it's in your best interest, always practice obedience.
5. Let others know when they've invaded your territory.
6. Take naps and always stretch before rising.
7. Run, romp, and play daily.
8. Eat with gusto and enthusiasm.
9. Be loyal.
10. Never pretend to be something you're not.
11. If what you want lies buried, dig until you find it.
12. When someone is having a bad day, be silent, sit close by and nuzzle them gently.
13. Delight in the simple joy of a long walk.
14. Thrive on attention and let people touch you.
15. Avoid biting when a simple growl will do.
16. On hot days, drinks lots of water and lie under a shady tree.
17. When you are happy, dance around and wag your entire body.
18. No matter how often you are criticized, don't buy into the guilt thing and pout.
19. Run right back and make friends.

Author Unknown
from *Chicken Soup for the Pet Lover's Soul*

Table 4.3
Insights from International Experiences
Nations visited by Dr. J. P. Eddy

Countries	Insights Gained
Iceland	This is the only nation I have known that teaches in its schools and colleges Icelandic, Danish, and English languages that students are required to learn. Here is also the oldest democracy in the world.
Philippine	This is a nation, I have seen, that has been impacted by the cultures of China, Spain, Saudi Arabia, American, and Japan, and they affect education on all levels.
Russia	This nation, I observed, has provided outstanding engineers and their accomplishments in space science projects.
Italy	This nation has produced many outstanding artists, and I have seen their marvelous paintings and art pieces in Rome, Italy.
Mexico	This nation, I have observed, has produced amazing calendars, sundials, temples, agriculture, and even a ball game thousands of years ago.
Japan	This nation, I have seen, has provided outstanding automobiles, beautiful gardens, and religious temples, fast rail trains, and good marshal arts programs for exercise.
India	This nation, I have observed, has produced beautiful buildings, excellent scholars in all fields, and world religions.
Israel	This nation, I have seen, has produced three world religions: Judaism, Christianity, and Islam.

Table 4.3 (continued)
Insights from International Experiences
Nations visited by Dr. J. P. Eddy

Countries	Insights Gained
Saudi Arabia	This nation, I have observed, has produced the Moslem religion, scientific contributions from Arabic scientists, and the largest oil reserves in the world.
Germany	This nation, I have observed, has produced famous scientists, musicians, theologians, military leaders, artists, engineers, and writers
England	This nation, I have seen, has produced famous leaders in human rights, science, navies, religion, and government.
Spain	This nation, I have seen, has beautiful cathedrals, fine art galleries, and excellent literature.
France	This nation, I observed, has fabulous museums, art galleries, architecture, rail trains, airplanes, and literature.
China	This nation, I observed, has contributed to world religions, gunpowder, art, architecture, literature, the Great Wall of China, successful capitalism in Hong Kong, moral leadership in government, world-class products, fireworks, and famous athletes.
Nigeria	This nation, I have observed, has provided famous leaders in all fields who succeed in many nations.

Women and Education in France
French Women in Higher Education

**Percentage of women among college
students in France (1996-97):**
56.0%

**Percentage of female students enrolled
in the following disciplines (1996-97):[1]**

* Languages   78.8%
* Literature—Linguistics—Art   74.4%
* Pharmacy   67.8%
* Humanities—Social sciences   65.1%
* Law—Political science   61.2%
* Administration   60.7%
* Natural sciences   56.0%
* Medicine   52.6%
* Economics—Business management   47.2%
* Dentistry   45.05
* Technical studies (2-year programs)   37.5%
* Sciences   35.1%
* Physical education   34.3%
* Technological science—Engineering   21.4%

Percentage of women in the teaching profession[2]

* Elementary level   76.0%
* Secondary level   56.2%
* Higher education   30.0%
    * assistant and associate professors   34.7%
    * full professors   13.0%

Measures Taken in France to Improve Education and Career Opportunities for Women

1. **Attraction to science and technology:**
   The French Ministry of Education has launched several campaigns since 1992 to encourage more female students (14-17 years old) to major in scientific and technical fields, using the slogan "C'est technique, c'est pour elle!" (It's technical, it for her)

2. **Selection of textbooks:**
   Special commissions were established to ensure that sexist stereotypes disappear from textbooks.

3. **Improvement of pedagogical practices:**
   Seminars have been organized so that teachers in scientific fields will avoid sexist practices and treat students of both genders in the same manner.

4. **Women's rights:**
   They are now part of the curriculum in all public middle schools all over France.

5. **Enforcing equality between men and women:**
   The reform of the education system that was enacted in 1989 included as one of its main objectives the enforcement of equality in education for men and women.

Women in France: Some Facts

Demographics

France: Population: 60 million (*fifth economic power in the world*)
                —51.3% of women

Divorce Rate: 30% (50% in large cities)

Fertility: 1.75% children per woman

Work Force: 86% of women 25-39 years old, 89% of women 40-49, 73% of women 50-59

Education

1882:   Education is free and mandatory for all children of both genders 6-13 years old
1924:   Common curriculum for students of both genders at the secondary level
1966:   Technical education open to women

Civil rights

1944:   French women have the right to vote
1965:   Married women may work and have a bank account without their husband's permission
1970:   Within a married couple, the father and mother share responsibility equally over the children
1975:   Divorce is allowed on mutual consent, without cause

Contraception

1967:   Contraception becomes legal; dissemination of the contraceptive pill
1975:   Contraception, including the pill, is covered by medical insurance; abortion becomes legal
1982:   Abortion is covered by medical insurance
1986:   The RU-486 abortive pill is developed in France

Work

1910:   Elementary school teacher receives a paid maternity leave
1928:   All female civil servants have a ten-week paid maternity leave
1945:   Mandatory maternity leave extended to all professions: 8 weeks with half salary
1966:   Paid maternity leave extended to 14 weeks for all working women
1980:   Paid maternity leave extended to 4 months for the first and second child, 6 months starting with the third child. In addition, a pregnant woman may not lose her job.
1983:   Law on professional equality: equal pay for equal work
1992:   Law of sexual harassment
1995:   Creation of the *Observatoire de la Parité* to check equality between genders.

Politics

1947: First woman as State Secretary (Germaine Poinso-Chapuis: Health and Population)
1970: *Mouvement de libération des Femmes* or *MLF* (Women's Liberation Movement)
1975: First woman as candidate for the presidential election (Arlette Laguiller)
1991: First woman Prime Minister (Edith Cresson)

Famous French Women and Pioneers

1903: Marie Curie receives the Nobel Prize in physics (with her husband Pierre).
1911: Marie Curie receives the Nobel Prize in chemistry.
1951: Jacqueline Auriol is the first female test pilot in the world.
1976: Valérie André is the first woman general in the French Air Force.
1993: First French woman astronaut (Claudie André-Deshaye); first woman as commander of a ship in the French navy.
1995: First woman as director of a nuclear plant in France.

The Internationalization of Corporations and Implications Worldwide

There are many international corporations that are controlling the former companies that were associated to one country. For example, here are illustrations in different nations worldwide:

1. Sweden: SAAB Car Corporation now is controlled by General Motors USA and Ford USA has bought Volvo Car Corporation.
2. Iceland: Coca-Cola Corporation in Iceland is controlled by Coca-Cola USA.
3. England: A number of publishing companies in England control some former USA publishing companies.
4. Japan: A number of banks owned by Japanese citizens control many banks across the world.

America's Shameful Treatment of Its Minority Citizens From 1619 to 1999

Native American Indians

Living on Indian reservations, I saw how our Native Americans were destroyed by European immigrants who brought their diseases of smallpox to kill them and alcohol or conquer them. Indians, who were the first Americans, didn't get voting rights until 1924, and all their treaties were broken to lose their lands.

African Americans

Living in Mississippi, I saw the tragedy of racial prejudice against African Americans as I taught at a Black Christian college in 1963. The injustices and denial of freedoms against African Americans who were here first in 1619 before the Pilgrims in 1620 is unbelievable.

Japanese Americans

Having Japanese students in my college courses, I learned of their internment in World War II and treatment as American citizens like enemies who bombed Pearl Harbor, Hawaii, on December 7, 1941. The Japanese youth who fought the Germans in Italy in World War II had one of the best records of any U.S. soldiers in that war. The African American fliers from Tuskegee had a great record against the Germans in World War II, too.

Mexican Americans

Having lived in New Mexico, I heard of the injustices against Mexican Americans who lost their land grants to white Anglo settlers after the Mexican-American wars of the 19th century. Thousands of Mexicans lost their land, and these lands are now owned by white Anglo settlers. Of course, these lands once owned by Mexican Americans were taken away first from the Native American Indians in the 16th century in New Mexico.

Summary

In America, we have seen discrimination against minorities such as I have mentioned here with regard to major groups of peoples such as

Native American Indians, African Americans, Japanese Americans, and Mexican Americans. However, I have also met other Americans from Jewish to Moslem peoples who tell me they have faced discrimination in America in my lifetime. Other ethnic and racial peoples have also shared stories of discrimination with me from the peoples of Asia to the peoples of Africa. The causes for discrimination appear to be having a different religion, a different language, a different color, and a different culture, which causes some Americans to act in a prejudiced behavior against other Americans.

Table 4.4
Comparing Freedoms of Women in American and Saudi Arabia: Selected Situations

Saudi Women (Moslems)	American Women (Christians or Other Religions)
Cannot drive a car in Saudi Arabia, but Saudi women defend this by saying they have their own private drivers for them.	American women can drive any vehicle and it's not against a law.
Saudi women cannot go to their husbands' work place, but their children can. Saudi women defend this by saying they know what their husbands do and they do not need to see them at their work site.	American women can go to any work site of their husbands unless it is a security situation of the government or law enforcement.
Saudi women often have servants from other nations take care of their children, do their housework, cook the family meals, and babysit while the Saudi women shop, go to school, and travel to various places in the country.	American women seldom have any servants to do childcare, housework, or babysitting.
Saudi women can hold jobs for pay outside the home, and servants cover for their home activities.	American women have the same opportunities, but few American women can afford servants to do their home jobs.

(continued)

Table 4.4 (continued)
Comparing Freedoms of Women in American and Saudi Arabia:
Selected Situations

Saudi Women (Moslems)	American Women (Christians or Other Religions)
Saudi women and men who study in their colleges or go overseas to other colleges get a free education and all expenses paid.	American women and men do not get this opportunity in our nation or overseas.
Saudi women are honored by Saudi men and are often treated like queens from my personal observations of Saudi families in America and in Saudi Arabia.	American women are sometimes treated like queens by American men, but it is rare from my observations over a 50-year period of clinical study in America.
Saudi women and men send their children to special daily religious schools besides their regular school that teaches the Islamic religion.	American women and men may once a week take their children to a Sunday school or religious class.
Saudi women and men are required in college work to take religion courses (Islamic faith).	American women and men who only attend some church-related college are required to take religion courses and these courses may teach more than one religion, not like the Saudi requirement of only one religion, that being Islam.

In Summary

I have been very impressed with the Saudi people I have known in their family behavior. For example, I have seen no alcoholics, smokers, child or spouse abusers, divorced families, or known of any criminals reported in the media of Saudi persons.

I only wish more American families were moral and ethical persons like these Saudi families that I have known. This comparison is given between Saudi and American persons to understand the differences between Saudi and American culture. At this time, Saudi Arabia and America are close allies in the world that both went through the Gulf War in 1991 together. American military forces are now in Saudi Arabia ready to be peacekeepers in the Middle East and to prevent violence between nations around the world.

Working to Eliminate Prejudice in America: Fourteen Programs in 1999

The following 14 programs Dr. Eddy is involved in to eliminate prejudices in America:

1. A T-shirt program to give away free T-shirts that have the following on the T-shirt: "Working for a prejudice free America" to leaders in American higher education.
2. A free picture of Dr. Martin Luther King, Jr. and President Mary McLeod Bethune to churches, schools, youth organizations, recreation centers, and social agencies that are involved in diversity education.
3. A free Gallery of Successful Americans in three buildings at the University of North Texas of minority persons and women.
4. A free in-service program for teaching persons to be better multicultural teachers and professors in schools and institutions of higher education in the North Texas Region.
5. A free multicultural diversity resource directory to persons that provide resources for programs for organizations, clubs, groups, churches, agencies, businesses, schools and colleges.
6. An Internet Project REAL that provides free computer information on opportunities for multicultural and diversity materials.

7. A <u>free volunteer service</u> Dr. Eddy gives as a storyteller to a child care center with children from five months to five years of age in Denton, Texas.
8. A <u>free volunteer service</u> Dr. Eddy gives to the Marcus Middle School of the Dallas Independent School District of Dallas, Texas as a special speaker to students, teachers and staff.
9. A <u>free volunteer service</u> Dr. Eddy gives to the Reconciliation Ministries of the Worldwide Church of God that has leaders from all religious groups throughout America who work for eliminating racism in America.
10. A <u>free volunteer service</u> Dr. Eddy gives to raising scholarship monies for minorities and women who are former U.S. military service personnel and military dependents to attend the University of North Texas as students.
11. A <u>free volunteer program</u> for speaking on children and youth suicide prevention and drug abuse education in schools, colleges, clubs and churches worldwide that Dr. Eddy does.
12. A <u>free breakfast program</u> Dr. Eddy offers via different organizations on prejudice free living for Americans to change our behavior from "racism" to "neighborism."
13. International and national <u>free conference programs</u> Dr. Eddy offers on university campuses throughout the world on diversity education.
14. <u>Volunteers</u> in several experiences on repentance of racism in worship services in relocation of the African American Community from the Civic Park in Denton, Texas to Southeast Denton, Texas. The segregation of African-Americans from St. Gregory's United Methodist Church in 1776 in Philadelphia, Pennsylvania at the St. James African Episcopal Methodist Church in Denton, Texas.

How Will America Get Along With Rival Nations in the 21st Century: Cooperation or Conflict?

Introduction

A key question for American citizens is how will our nation's leaders get along with the leaders of other nations across the world in the 21st century. Will there be peaceful cooperation or warlike conflict?

The rising military and economic force of China continues to be a threatening power to American. Again, the continued threats of Iraq to peace in the Middle East also threaten American allies there. Moreover, unsolved conflicts still exist in parts of Africa, Asia, South America, and Europe. America's role as a peacekeeper along with United Nations forces is a heavy burden to assume.

The American Volunteer Organizations

The generosity of America's volunteer organizations has saved the lives of thousands of children, youth and adults from death by starvation, disease, and disasters. American churches and humanitarian organizations have done what some nations refuse to do to save their own citizens.

America's Role as a Peacekeeper

America's role as a peacekeeper is an awesome burden. At this time, America's military forces are stretched to the uppermost with troop deployment in over 76 nations of the world. Our 1 ½ million military personnel are not enough to be police personnel and peace protectors in many nations.

What is the answer to a world gone wild with ethnic and religious groups that want their own piece of property in a new nation has yet to be determined. These ethnic and/or religious groups are often fighting within themselves for political power, economic advantage, and territorial possession.

With the availability of modern weapons and terrorist type technology, various groups of warriors are able to cause great turmoil with thousands killed annually and a society disturbed for years. Look at Cambodia, the Sudan, Columbia, Iraq, Kosko, and Indonesia, just to mention a few of the over 41 regional wars on planet earth.

Our prayers, our peaceful work, and our humanitarian aid programs help. But, this is not enough. People in all these warring nations must assume responsibility for killing persons and destroying property. This senseless behavior leads nowhere but to perpetate a "hell on earth" for the living death in those war zones across the globe.

Peace Teams Are Needed

Peace teams of persons are needed to stop wars, to treat the dying and injured by war, and to restore societies to a peaceful life. How this can be done is not clear at this period of history. However, it is needed and it is necessary, which all sane citizens would agree upon. Some of these problems worldwide that need attention are next mentioned.

Why Do We Still Have These Problems?

Why do we have prejudice, slavery, and killing in nations around the world in 1999?

1. In India in 1999, with its population of 1.2 billion of Indians, there are still more than 200,000 million untouchables—a cast system that keeps these people from having equal rights. Three thousand years of Indian history with the Hindu religion keeping the untouchables in their lowly status to live in slums, to bury the dead, to clean toilets, and to do the dirtiest jobs in India. While the president of India is now an untouchable, the untouchables are still being discriminated against. Upper class landlords keep untouchables as slaves working the farms. These landlords have even killed children, women, and men who are innocent persons as reported by "60 Minutes" on March 21, 1999. India claims it is the world's largest democracy, but it doesn't give freedom for its untouchables to be treated so immorally by the government and by the Hindu peoples of India.
2. In the Sudan, we have some children and women sold into slavery and working as slaves in 1999. This is hard to believe, but it is happening.
3. In Thailand, we have children being used as sexual prostitutes in 1999. These practices are criminal.
4. In Ruanda, some persons are still being killed by the Hutsie and Tutsie tribes that fight each other in 1999. Millions have been killed and crippled in the 1990s.

Why We Can't Ignore International Connections In Denton, Texas, or Anywhere Anymore

Here are a few selected facts on the impact of international students, citizens, and businesses related to Denton, Texas:

1. More than 1,200 international students are in full-time study at the University of North Texas and more than 600 international students are at Texas Woman's University.

2. An additional 330 international students take English as a Second Language course at the University of North Texas each year.

3. The economic impact of international students attending higher education institutions in Denton is more than $15 million per year, not counting tuition and fees of the institutions of higher education.

4. More than 300 University of North Texas students study abroad each year in 15 countries.

5. Professors and staff at the University of North Texas have projects and programs going in many nations.

6. The biennial Physics Accelerated Conference at the University of North Texas draws more than 800 scientists, engineers, governmental employees, and business personnel worldwide from about 47 nations to Denton, Texas.

7. The Thai Development Fund at the University of North Texas funds international projects worldwide each year for about $15,000 in several nations.

8. The most serious international effort is with Mexican colleges, universities and governmental agencies with more than 200 students, faculty, and staff involved in several Mexican geographical locations.

9. For every house we build in Denton with Habitat for Humanity, we build one home in Mexico—13 homes in Denton and 13 in Mexico.

10. In several University of North Texas graduate departments, the largest number of ethnic students are Chinese, to add a footnote to the fact that one out of four persons in the world is Chinese.

11. America's role as peacekeeper in the world affects our college's role in the world, too. Recently, on November 18, 1998, a program was held called International Day at UNT, which illustrated this situation via 22 exhibits.

12. The employment of many professors and staff at the University of North Texas depend on the number of international students who attend the University of North Texas in 1998-99.

13. Scores of our University of North Texas faculty and staff are former citizens of another country. These full-time employees are working in programs or teaching academic credit courses in education, business, physics, chemistry, music, political science, history, sociology, anthropology, library information science, computer education, biology, and other disciplines. These instructors come from Spain, India, Palestine, China, Hong Kong, Taiwan, England, Ireland, Cuba, the Czech Republic, Germany, Poland, Ukraine, Mexico, Iran, Columbia, South Korea, Ghana, Russia, and other nations.

14. The Higher Education area of the Department of Counseling, Development and Higher Education once had 25 percent of its students from abroad. We were enrolling more than 200 graduate students each academic term, which means about 50 were international students at that time to keep at least four faculty we do not have now employed. In other words, we had eight faculty then, and we have but four full-time faculty now.

15. The Center for the Study of Work Teams at the University of North Texas offers conferences each year that bring persons together from countries of the world, such as Mexico, Canada, Australia, Japan and others.

Notes

1. *Repéres et références statistiques sur les enseignements et la formation* (Paris: Ministére de l'Education nationale, de la Recherche et de la Technologioe, 1997), p. 151.
2. Nicole Mosconi. *Egalité des sexes en éducation et formation* (Paris: PUF, 1998), pp. 87-88.

Chapter 5

ΣΟ ΟΖ

Research Studies Published on Higher Education Worldwide

Introduction

The following selected research studies are coauthored articles on higher education subjects from 20 countries or territories around the world and published in seven different refereed journals in America and other nations. This chapter represents research done overseas from 1974 to 1994 in annotated style. These studies cover both the academic and student affairs areas on five continents.

England, France, Germany, Switzerland, Italy, Romania, Yugoslavia, Spain, Canada and the U.S.A.

Eddy, J. P. (1975). Towards an ideal international peace education conference to actualize selected educational principles. *Peace Progress Journal.* 1(1), 97-107.

This study presented materials from Canada, the U.S.A. and eight European countries that the author traveled to in 1974 gathering peace education information. It provides ideas and methods for the planning of peace education conferences in higher education institutions worldwide based on successful conferences and research experiments of the past.

Republic of China (Taiwan)

Eddy, J. P. and Chen, C. K. (1989). The dean of students in the Republic of China: Guardian of culture and freedom. *National Association of Student Personnel Administrators Journal.* 26(4), 295-299.

This study presents the history, job description, position philosophy and selected interview information of deans of students in the Republic of China (Taiwan). A dean of students in Taiwan, according to University Law (Article 15), should be a professor who has been certified by the National Ministry of Education as they head the Office of Discipline or Office of Dean of Students in their college or university.

Eddy, J. P., Chen, C. K, and Bell, J. L. (1988). Historical development of the Dean of Students. *College Student Affairs Journal.* 8(3), 4-10.

This study presented a historical review of both the academic dean and the dean of students in America. Recent studies of the dean of students from America to the Republic of China (Taiwan) are mentioned to point to the growing administrative aspect of the student personnel administrator position in higher education institutions.

Kenya

Maronga, G. B. and Eddy, J. P. (1994). Conditions in higher education in Kenya. *College Student Journal.* 28(1), 88-90.

This study presented historical background on the establishment of four national universities in Kenya. It gave information on the current status of higher education in Kenya and suggestions on how university administrators might meet the changes facing institutions there. Maronga's research on the deans of students in public universities was mentioned and how deans perceived themselves differently in their administrative behavior than their staff or college students.

Maronga, G. B.; Eddy, J. P.; and Spaulding, D. (1995). A national study of Kenya's public institutions' deans of students. *College Student Affairs Journal,* 15(1) 1-14.

This study presents the leadership behavior of the deans of students in Kenya's public universities. Significant differences were found among the perceptions of the deans of students (11 studied), student affairs staff (65 studied), and the student leaders (130 studied) regarding the real and ideal leadership behavior of the deans of students with regard to initiating structure and consideration—the two leadership dimensions surveyed with the Leadership Behavior Description Questionnaire.

Nigeria

Mallom, U. and Eddy, J. P. (1993). A study of polytechnic faculty turnover at selected Nigerian institutions. *College Student Journal.* 27(4), 523-524.

This study presented historical background and important information on the results of a survey of 247 full-time faculty from ten selected colleges of technology/polytechnics in Nigeria. The research revealed that among full-time faculty members present pay, opportunities for promotion, and lack of commitment to the institution are perceived to be the most influential factors concerning their colleagues' voluntary turnover.

South Korea

Lee, S. K. and Eddy, J. P. (1993). South Korean national study of junior colleges. *College Student Journal.* 27(3), 362-364.

This study presented an analysis of 44 of the 114 junior college presidents in South Korea as to their identification of current problems and future plans for resolving these problems in their institutions. Recommendations for future improvement of these two year colleges included adressing the following issues: financial difficulties, weekend colleges, negative public attitudes, cooperative education, integrity and autonomy of junior colleges, transfer difficulties, associate degrees, continuing education, and curriculum revision.

Thailand

Eddy, J. P. and Essarum, C. C. (1989). Student and faculty perception of a university academic advising process. *College Student Affairs Journal,* 9(2), 6-13.

This study presents survey data from 230 faculty advisors and 561 college students on how college student advisement is perceived in one of the world's largest universities located in Thailand. The results indicate a serious problem exists in advisement and that steps need to be taken to correct this problem.

Jordan

Sammour, H. Y. and Eddy, J. P. (1994). The first university in Jordan: The University of Jordan. *College Student Journal.* 28(2), 244-247.

This study presented research evidence on the first university in Jordan, the University of Jordan, which was founded in 1962. The article covered the historical development of the university, and it analyzed some of its educational practices to offer recommendations to improve its approaches.

Saudi Arabia

Own, Wafa M. and Eddy, J. P. (1992). Perception of Saudi women toward Saudi universities. *College Student Journal.* 26(3), 330-331.

This study presented research on two female institutions of higher education in Jeddah, Saudi Arabia: King Abdul Aziz University and the College of Education for Girls. An instrument was used to obtain the perception of 374 female students on 54 different activities. The results indicated there was a significant similarity in the students' rankings of the 54 activities.

United Arab Emirates

Eddy, J. P. and Sayah, E. N. (1988). The first national University of the United Arab Emirates. *Journal of Abstracts in International Education.* 17(1), 65-70.

This study presented research on the first university in the United Arab Emirates named the First National University of the United Arab Emirates that was founded in 1977 in Al-Ain. The article gave a historical background and a description of its status from academic curriculum to student composition.

Khlaifat, A. S. and Eddy, J. P. (1993). College students and student services in the United Arab Emirates. *College Student Journal.* 27(1), 143-144.

This study presented historical background and information on the college students and student services on the National University of the United Emirates at Al-Ain founded in 1977. Information on the University included admissions requirements, enrollment records, advising programs, student services, and recommendations for the improvement of student affairs.

Guam

Santos, R. D. and Eddy, J. P. (1993). Faculty and administrators' job preferential determinants at the University of Guam. *College Student Journal,* 27(4), 472-475.

This study presented research based on the surveys of 91 faculty members and 32 administrators at the University of Guam who completed a two-page paired comparison questionnaire. The results revealed that faculty members and administrators present a degree of disagreement among ranked factors and a degree of importance factors in their employment insight and job identity decision making process.

Columbia

Cabrales, E. J. and Eddy, J. P. (1992). Informatics education in Columbia. *Journal of Information Science*. 18(3), 217-224.

This study presented the results of research on the status of computer education in universities in Columbia. The results indicated an emphasis in undergraduate education and a lack of graduate programs. Computer companies need to play a more important role in providing up-to-date computers and scholarships in the computer science curriculum in the universities.

Cabrales, E. J. and Eddy, J. P. (1992). Evaluation of the actual state of information in Columbia. *Acucnoticias Journal*. 19(136), 1-6.

This study presented the challenges of the computer industry in Columbia and the needs of higher education with regard to the computer science curriculum. Recommendations were made to correct problems in colleges and universities in Columbia.

Chapter 6

ഇറ

International Research Studies and Other Common Concerns

O ver the years, the lead author has coauthored over thirty research studies overseas in higher education institutions in over twenty countries. These studies produced common concerns such as:

1. Faculty studies found common problems of low salaries and inadequate resources for teaching;
2. Dean of students studies found deans perceiving themselves more effective with students than were judged by students, faculty or staff colleagues;
3. Student services studies found a lack of student involvement in student activities;
4. Newly founded institutions of higher education from Thailand to Saudi Arabia have provided, since World War II, educational opportunities using distance education for these countries never before available to these people;
5. A study of two year colleges in South Korea found that more private junior colleges are proportionally in this country than any nation of the world in a nation that is second only to the U.S.A. in high school graduates going to college.

6. A study of computer education needs in Columbia found that higher education institutions need more financial and computer support from computer companies that have the wealth to do it;

7. A study of administrators in Nigeria found that tribal political considerations determined some university presidential leadership;

8. A study of colleges in Jamaica provides valuable insights into how a private institution of higher education can support itself with student and staff involved in growing agricultural crops;

9. A study of higher education in Guam points out the difficulty of recruiting and holding faculty in remote areas of the world; and

10. A study of higher education in Nepal indicated how in some nations the highest leaders of that nation are overly involved in their colleges and universities.

Surveying for a Generation Label

Recently, I did a survey of college students from 20 to 50 years of age on what generation they best identified with now. The responses came back as: "the me generation," "the X generation," "the lost generation," "the nameless generation," "the silent generation," and so forth. In probing into the values of students of different generational labels, similar values appeared such as: blaming others for their problems, abusing drugs, putting pleasure before principles, cheating in courses and on civil records and being irresponsible. Apparently, these generational labels are not descriptive nor fair to a generation of students. Again, other students across the generational labels have such values as: caring for persons, serving needy persons, volunteering for useful courses, upholding academic honor codes, abstaining from drug use, telling the truth in college and society, and being responsible. It is a media myth to stereotype any student generation.

College Student Affairs Leads the World

There is no doubt that college student affairs in the United States leads the world in providing valuable student development and services for higher education students. These opportunities for college students cover the development of mental, moral, physical, social, and spiritual aspects of their life. It is unfortunate more students do not take advantage of these opportunities for their total life development as they attend college.

Harassment Avoidance in Higher Education

Harassment in higher education, be it sexual, racial or circumstantial, has no place in a college or university. Prejudice, discrimination or bias toward persons should not happen on a college campus if students and staff are properly educated through in-service training and credit courses about their behavior and attitudes toward others different than themselves. The college or university should be a model community where everyone is given respect and acceptance regardless of their differences and where tolerance is observed. The values that need to be taught in both public and private schools are those that affect our behavior toward others such as kindness, tolerance, honesty, cooperation, nonviolence, encouragement, friendship and drug-free characteristics. In "directed dyads," these values are stressed so students can learn to be "value added persons" in college and for life.

New Internationalism in Higher Education

There is a new emphasis on internationalism at colleges and universities attributed to: the higher volume of international student exchange between the United States and other countries; the additional nonwestern courses on culture, history and politics; and the increase of foreign travel and business ventures by Americans around the world. As a result, foreign language course enrollments have increased in high schools and in colleges in especially certain languages such as Russian, Chinese and Japanese.

A study from the United States Office of Educational Research and Improvement of US based corporations employing over 400,000 people, has found:

1. An emphasis on students taking multiculturalism and diversity in college curricula and cultural activities is favored by employers; and
2. Corporations value a secondary language proficiency more highly than in the past and urge students to acquire these

language skills *[OER] Education Research Report,* (July, 1994), OR 94-3215, ED/OERI 938.

Trends in International Education Programs Abroad and Foreign Students Studying in USA

Some trends in higher education as it relates to international students studying in the USA and international programs abroad are:

1. More and more foreign students chose the USA to study in than any other country, resulting in 400,000 students from around the world studying within the USA in 1994;
2. International programs sponsored by USA higher education institutions overseas are fairly stable, but in certain countries such as Japan, USA colleges and universities are closing their branch campuses because the Japanese government is not accrediting them;
3. USA foreign students and staff exchanges are growing especially in former and present communist countries;
4. Japanese investors continue to buy small American liberal arts colleges that would have closed or combined with other American universities;
5. Women college students in some Moslem countries are demanding more opportunities for their education and employment;
6. College graduates across the world are having trouble finding employment in their major and minor areas of specialty. Thousands of these college graduates are coming each year to the USA, enrolling in our graduate schools, obtaining "green cards" for employment, and preparing to become naturalized US citizens;
7. College students continue to wield tremendous political power in some countries, especially those who are full-time students and have the time to protest against a government's policies. Nations where this is happening are South Korea, Nigeria, France, Indonesia, and Palestine's West Bank;
8. Where communism has diminished since 1990 in countries across the world, great changes have occurred in higher education institutions such as:

a) Professors with only Marxist orientation, for example, in the former East Germany have lost their positions and/or they have had to teach different courses with less Marxist doctrine;

b) In some nations, such as Romania, some professors with communist party membership were found also to be working for the Russian KGB (secret police) and they have been punished for their affiliation with foreign spies.

9. There are nations around the world, more liberal than the United States, where religious groups use public television and radio to present their beliefs such as Nigeria and the Philippines. Apparently, these governments interpret freedom for religion not freedom from religion as being in their national interest so their higher education institutions also have similar views;

10. Across the world there are "governments in exile" only waiting for the fall of a nation to move back to take over higher education and other institutions. Examples are the Cubans in Florida waiting for the collapse of Cuba and the Iranians in France waiting for the changes to happen in Iran;

11. Increasingly, Black institutions of higher education in the US are trying to make connections with colleges and universities in African countries for staff exchanges, cultural programs and research projects; and

12. International communication between personnel in higher education institutions is increasing dramatically due to Internet computer and FAX machine use so the world is becoming more of a global village every day.

References

Eddy, J. P. (1993). Higher education perspective for leadership. Edina, Minnesota: Burgess International Publishers.

Eddy. J. P. and Spaulding, D. (1994). International peace through higher education: the Senator J. William Fulbright Grants Program. *Peace Progress Journal,* 20(1), 1-6.

Egar, E. E. and Eddy, J. P. (1992). Factors contributing to the closing of Bishop College. *Negro Educational Review,* 62(3-4), 25-30.

Gunn, P. W. and Eddy, J. P. (1993). AIDS policies of Texas colleges. *Journal of college Student Development,* 34(2), 138-143.

Chapter 7

ഇറദ

Involvement and Learning of Higher Education Worldwide

Higher education faculty and staff need to get out of their ivory towers and out where the needs of the world are. The authors believe involvement in the problems of society brings colleges together in cooperative work with communities and even foreign countries to resolve these problems. For example, the lead author has discovered how this joint effort works as follows:

1. A visit to an Indian reservation in a work camp in Oklahoma in 1986 helped me understand the problems of alcoholism and drug addiction among Native Americans. Doing manual labor, from repairing to painting, with these Indians brought us closer together.
2. A visit to Saudi Arabia in 1992 helped me see the results of the Gulf War in the Middle East stated by Iraq with its invasion of Kuwait.
3. A visit to Guam in 1992 aided me to grasp the effects of World War II upon the population that suffered under Japanese occupation.

4. Attending an AIDS seminar service in 1993 in a Denton, Texas hospital and hearing HIV and AIDS patients tell how they got AIDS while attending institutions of higher education helped me understand how drug abuse can lead to HIV and AIDS disease.

5. Participating in a response session in the Dallas, Texas KRLD radio series on "Teenagers, Drinking and Driving" in 1994 presented opportunities to work on high school and college student alcohol abuse and misuse problems in Texas.

6. Raising a question in the "North American Violence in the Media Teleconference" that reached 130 cities in the United States and Canada in 1994 opened my mind to the complex and confusing issues of violence in American films and on American television. For example, I learned that American public school children from K to 12 grades see, in 13 years, over 15,000 hours of television in their homes with an average of 250,000 acts of violence in films viewed. On the other hand, these same children attend their schools from K to 12 grades for 12,000 hours and only 44 hours are devoted to health education to avoid drugs and to have good exercise and food habits. Is it any wonder some of our children and youth in America are in turmoil?

7. Presenting a 1994 session on "American Heroes" at the annual Young Peoples University at the University of North Texas guided me in observing how youth are lacking heroes that give them moral, ethical and practical role models for living a good life.

8. Giving several presentations of self-directed work team research on "directed dyad" in college residence halls from Fairbanks, Alaska to Minneapolis, Minnesota and Austin, Texas, in 1994, offered me insights on how higher education personnel desire better ways to impact college students that affects positively their holistic development.

9. Hearing the stories, in 1994, of persons who are from Russia, Estonia, Iraq, Zaire, Cuba and Haiti who have seen the negative results of communism, fascism, tribalism and individualism in these countries enlightened me. The stories of violence and vulgarity in these nations is sad, sinful and shameful. Thousands of Rwadan citizens fled to Zaire when

over a million Rwadan children, youth and adults were killed by tribal conflicts in that country in 1994-95.

10. Viewing films from around the world in 1994 and seeing the problems caused by humans of environmental losses from destroyed forests to polluted waters and air has caused a sensitivity towards preserving the earth's resources.

11. Visiting, in 1994, with former higher education doctoral students and colleagues of mine has been most revealing. One must actively listen to persons in order to learn of their accomplishments and experiences. For example, Dr. Ray Toledo, psychologist, medical doctor and professor of psychology at the University of North Texas shared with me a ten year project he has been leading in Mexico in the summers. This project has done the following: 1) Helped a Mexican city gain volunteer time on resolving some of its health and medical problems; 2) Provided college students with a valuable internship in a multicultural setting for a university course credit. Again, a visit with Dr. Paul Jacobs, who taught in the Philippines in 1993-94, revealed his insights into the multicultural problems developing nations faced with issues of hunger, shelter, unemployment and tribal wars. Moreover, a visit with Dr. Dale Rorex, who has a position with a Japanese university and has taught multicultural courses in Japan for several years, revealed how Japanese leaders are supporting multicultural credit courses in their higher education institutions so their college students are informed of other cultures around the world and how to deal with persons from different cultures. Finally, a visit with Dr. Edward N. Sayah, who is a consultant with the Saudi National Guard and an American citizen with Ph.D.'s from the University of North Texas and Oxford University, helped me see how difficult world conditions are to stop wars and to keep peace between nations.

12. Working with Lt. Col. U.S. Army (Retired) Donald Spaulding on veterans issues in America from the lack of higher education funds for recent veterans to the Gulf War Syndrome of veterans. Colonel Spaulding spent nearly 30 years in the U.S. military service: fighting in wars in Vietnam and Panama; working in the Pentagon; and teaching ROTC college

credit courses. In his travels, in over 50 nations of the world, he has seen many cultures and peoples. Some insights from his U.S. military research reveal: 1) The U.S. armed services is one of the least prejudiced work places in our nation now; and 2) More minorities can gain leadership opportunities in this American institution than in almost any organization in the country today.

13. Dr. Paul D. Jacobs, a former doctoral student of mine, who went to the Philippines from 1993 to 1994 to teach in a seminary under the Foreign Mission Board of the Southern Baptist Convention provided many insights into jobs overseas. Some of his observations are most helpful such as the hundreds of teaching jobs that are available overseas. Dr. Jacobs told me how hard it is finding teaching jobs in America in some fields due to a surplus of graduates and a shortage of positions. His research has found that being a Teaching Fellow does not count as much as it used to due to the strong competition in some fields.

Chapter 8

୫୦୦ଛ

Why Higher Education Cannot Avoid the World's Problems

Introduction

The reasons higher education cannot avoid the world's problems lie in the lessons of history. For example, throughout history the great progress of learning and development of libraries storing this knowledge has often been lost due to wars and the results of wars. From the burning of the library in Alexandria, Egypt in 47 B. C., during the siege of Julius Caesar, to the bombing of universities by many nations in World War II from 1939 to 1945, huge losses have been suffered worldwide due to wars. In the case of the Alexandria Library, started in the 200's B. C. period under the Egyptian ruler Ptolemy I, this library was the largest and most famous of all the ancient book collections in the world up to that time. At one time, over 500,000 books were held at the library before it was destroyed.

Higher Education Institutions Need Higher Priorities

In America, the highest priority of some universities is that they have a winning football or basketball team above all else. Coaches are hired at the highest salaries given any administrator or faculty member at some universities. If the coach doesn't win, he or she may even have his or her contract bought out even if it costs hundreds or thousands of dollars to settle the case. By all measures of higher education priority, this shows how far some universities will go to have a winning basketball or football team. Universities will put up with more financial losses, ethical and legal scandals for athletics than for any other area or issue at an institution and more discipline problems with students and coaches (staff). If this isn't the highest priority for scholarship athletics, above all else including academics, what is this all about? The problem is, we have become so used to these legal, ethical and moral scandals in scholarship athletics, we no longer challenge the system that perpetuates this insane illness and the losses of integrity.

What are the higher priorities of life? Certainly, the highest priority of life should be the saving of one's life from death or injury (physically or psychologically) (Eddy and Madden, 1975). The highest priority of life, then, theologically, philosophically and logically should be to save lives from death or injury. By the way, college football has its share of deaths and injuries each year and by changing rules for it we would save many lives from death and lifelong painful injuries. As a former college basketball player and college basketball coach, I know something about this subject. I still feel a football injury I suffered in high school, 44 years ago.

The Highest Priority is Lifesaving

If we believe lifesaving is the highest priority, then, we should do what the Jimmy Carter Center at Emory University attempts to accomplish, such as attempts at preventing terrorism, undemocratic leadership and wars worldwide. The authors believe colleges and universities across the world ought to have peace education centers to train students in all disciplines concerning how to combat violence in nonviolent approaches to stop killings and wars around the world.

What Universities Can Do

Universities can do great things if they have great leadership. Leadership is lacking at many universities. Some university leaders are more concerned about their athletic team being number one than having good academic programs. The energy and time off of many university staff at some institutions is devoted to athletic fund raising and publicity promotion of their athletic programs.

By establishing peace education centers like the Jimmy Carter Center at Emory University, universities are doing things that save lives and make a more peaceful, progressive, prosperous and productive world. The lead author helped start such a center at Felician College in Chicago, Illinois (Eddy and Jaski, 1975). Our priorities must change, or we will destroy ourselves like the Romans who put their Coliseum sports before the saving of their empire. Having seen the ruins of the Coliseum in Rome, I believe someday in the future, scholars will look at the ruins of our great sports stadiums and say, "history repeated itself."

References

Eddy, J. P. and Jaski, E. (1975). Felician College: the international peace center. *Peace Progress Journal.* 1(1), 65-66.

Eddy, J. P. and Madden, M. (1975). Peace education through an international dimension. *Peace Progress Journal.* 1(1), 71-76.

Chapter 9

ನ಼ಌ

Preventing Parental Malpractice Worldwide: A Higher Education Resolution

Abstract

Preventing criminal parenting worldwide is an article on how persons can stop the violence of parents against their children and the violence of children raised in parent abusing families. Of course, the authors will prefer persons lived by love and not the letter of the law, but abuse of children is killing our culture. The solutions suggested arise out of the licensing philosophy and practices of governmental units in states and/or countries. Philosophy for this comes from worldwide religious ideology and legal jurisprudence over the ages. Precedence already exists for all of the suggestives offered here so nothing new is being offered except for the saving of our children's lives and health. All ideas here have been advocated by others so credit should go to many persons.

Introduction

The reports of millions of children abused by parents abound across the world's media. From Rwanda in Africa to New York City in America, we hear of how cruel parents are doing criminal acts against children. How can we eliminate or at least reduce this criminal behavior? If laws were passed and enforced in our nations on child abuse, millions of abusing parents would face malpractice parenting charges much as medical doctors who abuse their patients or counselors abuse their clients. These abusing parents would be jailed, fined, and required to attend parenting skills courses and counseling therapy sessions for their abusive behavior.

Resolution of Parental Malpractice

The resolution of parental malpractice in America and in other countries might take the following philosophy and practice of governmental licensing from agencies across the world. In many nations, persons must have a driver's license to drive a vehicle; a hunting license to hunt wildlife animals or birds; a professional license to practice a particular occupation; and a health license to open an eating establishment. With this kind of precedence in law for all of these licenses, one must have a parental license to have children. The cost of the parental license will pay for the license costs of other licenses. Let us take actual license policies from these aforementioned licenses and apply them to the most precious person or possession that we have the privilege to have on this earth, our children (Eddy, 1994). These selected policies might be from these licenses:

1. **Parents must pass** health tests before they can have children, following the health license for eating establishments on good food and living environment.
2. **Parents must pass** mental tests on parenting attitudes and actions following the driver's license tests on the rules of the road.
3. **Parents must pass** gun tests before they have guns following the hunter's license tests for gun safety and treatment of animals with guns.
4. **Parents must pass** knowledge and ethics tests like those given for professional licenses in medicine or counseling.

Penalties for Parental Malpractice

Parents who do not take these enabling tests to get their parental license will be subject to many different penalties. They will not be able to do the following:

1. No welfare support will be provided them;
2. No health insurance will be offered them;
3. No vehicle licenses will be issued to them; and
4. No hospitals can fail to report them if they show up for medical aid without a parental license except in emergencies so no life is hurt.

The College of Parental Education

Across the world leaders would develop the newest educational institution entitled, the College of Parental Education (Eddy, 1994). This flexible institution of higher education would provide a series of courses for parents to take by "distance learning television," "correspondence courses" and "campus courses" on weekends. These courses will have special informative textbooks for the preparation of passing tests to get the parental license in each state or country. There will be fees for the courses, so they pay for themselves.

Content of Parental Courses

These courses would stress the positive exemplary parenting values such as being a drug free and role model parent who doesn't abuse his or her child. Other values that will be taught such as: respect and tolerance for children and adults; patience and love for children and adults; kindness and concern for children and adults; food, shelter, clothes, medical heath and education for children and adults. These values are based in U.S. Constitutional Law, the U.S. Bill of Rights, the U.S. Supreme Court approved laws and fifty state Supreme Court approved laws in the United States of America. These values will not compromise any citizen's rights so they cannot be suitable court cases to destroy teaching the values in these courses.

These courses will provide concrete content for the passing of these courses. The textbook can be used for life (Eddy, 1993) for each participant to develop good parenting skills. Opportunities for grandparenting courses will also be offered by the College of Parental Education, so parenting skills are offered from the cradle to the coffin.

Reporting Parental Malpractice

Those educated parents who have acquired the parental license will also be held accountable and creditable for their actions to their children. Persons who report abusing parents will have the protection of the government and will have income tax benefits. Those abusing parents who are reported by the public to have abused their children will face the following:

1. Their pictures will be published in local papers, after due process has found them guilty of crimes to children.
2. Their welfare support will be lost.
3. Their vehicles will be confiscated by the state for public auctions.
4. Their employers will be notified of their character malpractice.
5. Their parental license will be taken away.

Summary of the Article

This article has taken a stand against the abuse of children across the world because:

1. Parents without consciences have failed to be loving fathers and mothers to nurture their children in healthy homes.
2. Some religious groups have failed to teach their members to be faithful parents to children.
3. The governments have failed to put treating children on the same level as obtaining driver's licenses, hunting licenses, health licenses and professional licenses in society.

Therefore, the proposals in this article are not radical but go to the roots of what licenses do in many nations to hold persons accountable for their behavior.

Parent Effectiveness Training

Recently, Parent Effectiveness Training (PET) was required in the United States military. This is an eight hour unit taught by the chaplains corp. The lead author studied with Dr. Thomas Gordon, founder and author of the book, *Parent Effectiveness Training*. Dr. Gordon's method is one of the most widely accepted approaches in the field of parent education throughout the world.

References

Eddy, J. P. (1995). Parent Skill Courses Needed. Denton, Texas: Refereed paper presented at the First Annual Family Education Conference at University of North Texas.

Eddy, J. P. (1994). How can we stop violence in our cities? Dallas, Texas; National Teleconference on Media Violence.

Eddy, J. P. (1993). Violence prevention strategies in higher education and society. Denton, Texas: Lecture presented in EDHE 6510 Doctoral course.

Chapter 10

℘)(℃

Values for American Higher Education

Introduction

William Bennett's new book, *The Books of Virtues,* is an anthology of writings of other persons from Plato, the Greek philosopher, to Martin Luther King, the American clergyman and civil rights leader. Bennett (1993), Distinguished Fellow in the Cultural Policy Studies at the Heritage Foundation, selects ten virtues such as self-discipline, compassion, responsibility, friendship, work, courage, perseverance, honesty, loyalty, and faith for the benchmarks or standards to place the writings of over one hundred authors into these categories. Bennett believes these authors present important values to be taught in our families, schools, colleges and society. The authors agree with Bennett and include the supportive evidence of other lists of values from George Counts, former Professor at Southern Illinois University (S.I.U.), and John Eddy, former Professor at Loyola University of Chicago. Eddy studied under Counts at S.I.U. from 1965 to 1968 and took four courses from him where he emphasized these values.

The following chart presents values that should be taught in American higher education via the values lists of Counts, 1952; Eddy, 1977; and Bennett, 1993. In the chart, it is shown where these men have like type values in their lists. It is important to mention the following:

1. These values transcend gender, age, race, ethnicity and other factors that divide persons into labels and categories.
2. These values are stabilizing mechanisms for a blended American culture—a rainbow philosophy of diversity.
3. These values are cross-cultural or culturally universal or multicultural so they transcend independent cultures.
4. These values are critical to the survival of a multicultural society.
5. These values transcend religion, kinships, political systems, economic systems, ethnic customs and traditions even as they are derived from different cultural elements.
6. These values are cognitive and emotion based on being both implicit and explicit.
7. These values can be taught in higher education by: teaching both directly and indirectly; modeling by faculty staff and administrators; and participating in co-curricular and curricular activities by students and staff.
8. These values are ones that college students can learn, and where students are at an age where they can develop a life philosophy to practice and transfer these values to others to inculcate.
9. These values are often inherent in various religious dogma and doctrine.
10. These values can help bring persons together to heal, to help and to give hope in life.
11. These values help create a sense of community.
12. These values help contribute to a restoration and continued stability of community.

Table 10.1
Values for American Higher Education Chart

Counts (1952)	Eddy (1977)	Bennett (1993)
Hebraic-Christian ethic (Eddy, 1977) (Bennett, 1993)	Peace (Counts, 1952) (Bennett, 11993)	Self-discipline (Eddy, 1977) (Counts, 1952)
Humanistic spirit (Eddy, 1977) (Bennett, 1993)	Acceptance (Counts, 1952) (Bennett, 1993)	Compassion (Eddy, 1977) (Counts, 1952)
Science and scientific method (Eddy, 1977) (Bennett, 1993)	Concerned government (Counts, 1952) (Bennett, 1993)	Responsibility (Eddy, 1977) (Counts, 1952)
Rule of law (Eddy, 1977) (Bennett, 1993)	Healthy living environment (Counts, 1952) (Bennett, 1993)	Friendship (Eddy, 1977) (Counts, 1952)
Democratic faith (Eddy, 1977) (Bennett, 1993)	Faith or values to live by (Counts, 1952) (Bennett, 1993)	Work (Eddy, 1977) (Counts, 1952)
	Physical and mental heath (Bennett, 1993)	Courage (Eddy, 1977) (Counts, 1952)
	Meaningful marriage (Counts, 1952) (Bennett, 1993)	Perseverance (Eddy, 1977) (Counts, 1952)
	Meaningful occupation (Counts, 1952)	Honesty (Eddy, 1977) (Counts, 1952)
	Meaningful avocations (Counts, 1952)	Loyalty (Eddy, 1977) (Counts, 1952)
	Meaningful education (Counts, 1952) (Bennett, 1993)	Faith (Eddy, 1977) (Counts, 1952)

America Leads in Violence of Children and Youth

Violence statistics on children and youth in America are from the Children's Defense Fund and the Harvard School of Public Health, June, 1993.

1. Nine out of ten young people murdered in industrialized nations are murdered in America and of teenagers 15 to 19 years, one in four deaths come from a gunshot injury.
2. Nearly 50,000 children were killed by firearms between 1979 and 1991, which is equivalent to the number of American deaths in the Vietnam War.
3. A 79 percent increase of 10 to 17 year olds used firearms to commit murder between 1980 and 1990.
4. The third leading cause of death is homicide for elementary and middle school children from age 5 to 14 with 1 out of 5 male high school students in crime-ridden neighborhoods reported owning a gun.
5. In the past 25 years, over 800,000 Americans have died by guns which is more than two times greater than the number of American battle deaths in all of the foreign wars in the twentieth century.
6. A child growing up in America is 15 times as likely to be killed by gunfire as a child growing up in Northern Ireland with the average cost of firearm fatalities the highest of any injury related death at $373,000 per death.

Violence in Americas is no accident for it is the accumulation of long neglected problems: child abuse and family poverty; increasing economic inequality; racial intolerance and hate crimes; pervasive drugs and alcohol abuse; violence in our homes and popular culture; growing number of out-of-wedlock and teen births; more aggressive marketing of and easier access to deadlier firearms; hordes of lonely and neglected children and youths left to fend for themselves by absentee parents in all race and income groups (latch key kids); gangs of inner city and minority youths related to the lowest ring of society without adequate education, jobs, hope or an economic and social stake in our society; and governmental and societal misleadership on facing these problems in society. Statistics that validate the broken families of America are:

1. 27% of children under age 18 lived with one parent in 1993; in 1970 it was 12% of this 27%; 37% are children of divorce, 35% from never married parents.
2. 57% of black children live with one parent, 21% for whites, 32% for Hispanics.
3. 71% of all children under age 18 live with two parents in 1992; 8,596 in 1970.
4. 87% of single family parents are female; 13% male.

Unmarried couple households in 1970 was 523,000; 1993 it was 3.5 million.

America: A Violent Society

If ever a nation needed good values for its peoples, America is that country. Violence seems to permeate American society everywhere from the inner city public housing units to the college campus residence halls. When one studies criminal backgrounds, a common pattern seems to emerge of troubled youth whose neglectful parents failed to give them needed love, acceptance and good role models. The problem youth have often found mutual peers who are also angry and crazy with drugs and weapons. Then, the attack occurs on some victim over sex, money, possessions, power or nothing. Injury and even death happens because these youth have no good role models they will turn to for help or friendship. Americans who are victims of obsessive love, the preys of crazed substance abusers or simply in the wrong place at the wrong time are too often at risk in our society of violence.

Television and movies feed children, youth and adults with deadly daily doses of violence to cause persons to parrot persons who injure, cripple and kill persons. Guns and weapons, in spite of five day gun purchase delays, are readily available for persons to use. Drugs, legal and illegal, are everywhere to change the chemistry of persons into violent killing machines like the "Terminator."

Why Teaching These Values is Essential

The values mentioned in this article need to be taught to young children if persons are to change from violent criminals to responsible citizens. Families need to take leadership but in a nation where there are millions of single family parents, it is hard to discipline, nurture and guide children when the one parent is working outside the home.   Children turn to television as their babysitter seeing violence everywhere, and as they grow older, they may turn to gangs for their emotional support and drugs to escape from their pain.   Some youth get into selling drugs and theft in their gang activity which often leads to drive by shootings, drug abuse, criminal arrests and prison time.

The American public, through opinion polls, has identified violence as the number one problem in the nation.   For years, polls of school and college administrators have identified drugs and weapons with youth violence as the number one problem on their campuses .   The need for the teaching and modeling of key values in American higher education has been mentioned by Counts, 1952; Eddy, 1977; and Bennett, 1993. This country has one of the highest rates of family violence resulting in the need for teaching and modeling of key values for the survival of our people.   Strange in our nation that has provided more freedoms for its people than most nations that we suffer a severe shortage of the very values that our people need to survive.   Part of the problem exists in a misinterpretation of the Constitution on teaching religious values as freedom from religion rather than freedom for religion.   In public higher education, we have academic freedom to teach various values but not so in our public schools.   However, only in the private schools and colleges are religious values more likely to be taught.

Drugs Contribute to Bad Behavior

Alcohol and drug use are also contributing factors to violence cases. When a person is troubled he or she often abuses alcohol and drugs. These drugs distort perceptions and lessen inhibitors so distraught persons may look for a confrontation with other persons.

How Does One Develop A Positive And Tolerant Personality?

The values that Counts, 1952, Eddy, 1977, and Bennett, 1993 advocate need to be demonstrated by "positive and tolerant of other persons typed personalities."   Menninger, Mayman and Pruyser, 1963 covers the negativistic personality who says no to just about everything as "rigid, chronically unhappy individuals, bitter, insecure and often with suicidal" characteristics. Swindoll, 1990, has proposed that persons work on personality characteristics that bring prejudice and intolerance between persons. Swindoll, 1990, lists these actions of persons that keep millions in bondage such as: "legalism, expectations, traditionalism, manipulation, demands, negativism, control, comparison, perfectionism, competition, criticism, pettiness, and a host of others; and from within: pride, fear, resentment, bitterness, an unforgiving spirit, insecurity, fleshly effort, guilt, shame, gossip, hypocrisy, and so many more . . . grace killers, all!" Grace is meant by Swindoll to mean that unconditional love one lives towards another person or persons without any reward. This grace is like the hymn "Amazing Grace." Persons who exhibit grace, give an acceptance, love, warmth and compassion towards other persons. This is living out the values that Counts, 1952, Eddy, 1977, and Bennett, 1993, are approaching the value of religion in bringing persons together in peaceful, cooperative, and helpful ways.

The Value of Religion to Change Human Behavior

Over the centuries, history records the lives of thousands of persons who have been positively changed by a religious experience. The word religion has two Latin language roots that means "to bind up and to bring together things that are broken." If one looks at religion in this context, then, "the language of healing and the actions of healing are appropriate . . . and religion becomes a way of looking at the whole of life again" (Harpur, 1994). This is the way that Counts, 1952, Eddy, 1977, and Bennett, 1993, are approaching the value of religion in bringing persons together in peaceful, cooperative, and helpful ways.

Conclusion

This presented a rationale for teaching values in American higher education. It provided the value lists of Counts, 1952; Eddy, 1977; and Bennett, 1993. A chart compared how each of these men covered those values. The authors challenge higher education faculty, administrators and staff to teach these values in the college curriculum and extra-curriculum by word and deed (good role models).

References

Anderson, K. (July 20, 1994). "Single parents on the rise." *Dallas Morning News*. P. 1

Bennett, W. J. (1993). *The Book of Virtues*. New York, New York: Simon and Schuster.

Counts, G. S. (1952). *Education and American Civilization*. New York, New York: Bureau of Publications, Teachers College, Columbia University.

Eddy, J. P. (1977). *College Student Personnel Development. Administration and Counseling*. Washington, D. C.: University Press of *America*.

Harpur, T. (1994). *The uncommon touch: An investigation of spiritual healing*. Toronto, Canada: McClelland and Stewart Inc.

Menninger, K.; Mayman, M.; and Pruyser, P. (1963). *The vital balance*. New York: Viking Press, 204-205.

Swindoll, C. R. (1990). *The grace awakening*. Dallas, Texas: Word Publishing, 302.

Rogers, C. R. (1961). *On becoming a person*. Boston, MA.: Houghton-Mifflin Publishers.

―― (1993). "Cease fire in the war against children." Washington, D. C.: Children's Defense Fund.

―― (1993). "Violent crime summary of children and youth." Cambridge, MA: Harris Poll prepared for the Harvard University School of Public Health.

Chapter 11

৪০০৪

Issues in Multiculturalism in Higher Education: From Texas Colleges to the World's Universities

Abstract

Multiculturalism is a much maligned and misunderstood approach in American higher education which needs to be intelligently covered to use it wisely and carefully in college. The subject of multiculturalism is affecting many higher education institutions across the world from Texas colleges to the world's universities. From Dr. Martin Luther King, Jr., civil rights leader, to Dr. Julian Bond, History Professor at American University (Eddy, 1995), and from United Nations Ambassador Eleanor Roosevelt to U.S. Vice President Hubert Humphrey (Eddy, 1993) the lead author has interviewed some of the pioneers of the multicultural movement in the USA, and he brings this perspective to this lecture. Multiculturalism is affecting the higher education curriculum and extra curriculum from college students to student services and administration (hiring, tenure and advancement). How have the affects of past enslavement, racism, genocide, illiteracy and present negative living environment impacted American minorities? What should American higher education institutions do to redress the wrongs of the past to minorities and what are the problems in implementing multiculturalism short of academic revisionism? The issues of minorities and their impact upon academic credit course content to specific student activities funding are serious conflicts on many college campuses. What are the rational, emotional, and spiritual advantages and disadvantages of applying multicultural models at colleges and universities from the USA to Japan (Eddy, 1995)? The chief investigator and research presenter here has dealt with the malaise of multicultural education for over 40 years from the Philippines (1954) to Saudi Arabia (Eddy, 1994) so he will share a number of actual case studies (pros and cons) on these multicultural experiences. The key issues of teaching, course testing, I.Q. testing, freedom of speech, academic freedom, minority rights and good taste behavior of citizens' needs to be clarified. In conclusion, multicultural-ism—regardless of its opposition—is sweeping across selected universities of the world. It is important for higher education boards of regents, administrators, faculty, staff and students to understand the ideal values and real challenges of multiculturalism and its broadest implications for democracy in America from the U.S. constitution applications, U.S. Supreme Court decisions and controversial political correctness situations on college campuses.

Introduction: Multiculturalism In American Higher Education: Roots, Rights and Reactions

Few issues in American higher education in this century have caused more disagreements than implementing multiculturalism in the curriculum and extra curriculum. The historical roots of American democracy in the U.S. Declaration of Independence, the Bill of Rights and the Constitution gave our country a paper democracy of rights. It took the American Civil Rights Movement of the 1960's to make these paper rights realities in voting, use of public facilities, and access to employment, housing as well as all areas of American life. Multiculturalism and political correctness has followed the implementation of the Constitution's paper rights along with the support of key Supreme Court decisions. American higher education, from the beginning, has been a pioneer as well as a battleground over how these rights by minorities are actualized. Private colleges have often been leaders in racial relations whereas some public universities have had severe problems with racial, ethnic and gender tolerance using academic freedom and the freedom of speech as covers for prejudice and harassment.

The University of North Texas has been a leader in Texas and the South in being innovative, creative and productive in providing multicultural curriculum and extra curriculum programs. There are a number of multicultural models which are operating in American higher education which need to be identified.

Purposes

1. To give a brief historical background to multiculturalism in American higher education.
2. To present the pros and cons of issues in multiculturalism in the curriculum and extra curriculum in colleges and universities in America.
3. To provide successful multicultural models in higher education worldwide.
4. To inform how the University of North Texas has been a leader in some aspects of multicultural work in curriculum and extra curriculum programs.
5. To identify ways how American higher education can be constructive, instructive, and productive in multiculturalism into the 21st Century to make American democracy a reality for all Americans.

The problem of dealing with prejudice towards a person or group of persons is an issue of how does one become more tolerant of persons who are different by race, ethnicity, gender, sexual orientation, disability, religion, economic status, political affiliation or whatever characteristics that divide a person's acceptance to another person as an acceptable human being. The multicultural movement attempts to educate persons to be more tolerant and less prejudice. Research on dealing with AIDS persons indicate "increased knowledge must not be regarded as a comprehensive solution for the dilemma of treating AIDS families. Thus, it is important to supplement a strong knowledge base with a variety of other potentially enhancing factors, such as increased contact, small group interactions, examination of stereotypes, and affective considerations which may all contribute to positive therapeutic experiences" (Green and Bobele, 1994). The authors' experience and clinical observations in dealing with persons of different background relates to these research conclusions. Simply stated what is evident here is that academic studying of different typed persons is not enough to change one's bias towards those different persons. It takes making friends with these different persons to really discover how prejudices are eliminated or lessened (Pleck, O'Donnell, O'Donnell and Snarey, 1988). Educators who teach multicultural courses and lead multicultural activities to reduce prejudice between different types of groups need to take this research into consideration for effective program leadership (extra curricular) and classroom teaching (curriculum).

In context to developing friendships with persons of different backgrounds, a person working in higher education should join organizations that have more minority persons (Eddy, 1977) if one wants to make friends with his or her fellow professionals. For example, the National Association of Student Personnel Administrators (NASPA), in its 1993-94 annual report, stated, "currently, 16 percent of NASPA members identify themselves as either Asian American, African American, Hispanic or Native American. Of those, an increasing number serve in leadership positions at both the national and regional levels" [*National Association of Student Personnel Administrators 1993-94 Annual Report.* (1994). Washington, D.C.: National Association of Student Personnel Administrators Publishers].

There are a number of themes that encompass the philosophy of the National Council for Accreditation of Teacher Education standards that support multiculturalism such as high quality, collaboration, diversity, intellectual vitality, performance expectations, programs evaluation and technology. The self-directed work team, the "directed dyad," is a method the authors use in their courses to reduce prejudices of working with persons of culturally diverse and exceptional populations. Again, the authors use case studies in these dyads to develop critical thinking, problem-solving and performance skills based on knowledge of content areas, the community; the college context, curriculum goals, and federal-state laws that impact higher education.

There are scholars who see the majority of American education as highly ethnocentric, and some have a tendency to teach as if the mainstream culture were the right and only one. Multicultural education is provided to enrich our understanding and tolerance of persons of different backgrounds. Students who are ostracized in schools and colleges because of their differences need special student services support. The college core curriculum needs to emphasize that culture, gender, economics, and language are dimensions of a student's personal culture and identity which will influence a student's approach to change to be educated and to live on campus. It is important to understand a college student's needs and to develop collaborative approaches to meet these needs through planned intervention, preventative education and personal cooperation and appropriate counseling.

In summary, some scholars would hold to an ethnocentric position for teaching higher education from the bias of a singular cultural mode. Other scholars would follow a multicultural approach drawing from alternative theories, models and practices from a number of cultures using culture as a core concept for all interpersonal interactions. Multicultural education is held here as a mediating, liberating and explanatory pedagogy in this content and context in the college classroom.

Nevertheless, political correctness, which is a natural by-product of multicultural education, has in 1994 gone far beyond the college campus. When the national U.S.A. mass media reports the alleged racist remarks of a minority professional football coach—"He is just another white quarterback"—it's national news. The public hears the reverse discrimination, repercussions, repressions and reprimands of the football coach. One single sentence using but one descriptive adjective identifying race—"white"—was used. Of course, "just another" was said before "white" so a group incrimination here is presented by the football coach. The recent movie, "White Men Can't Jump," seems racist by its title using this criterion of sensitivity but is there a place for ethnic humor or satire in our American culture anymore? That key question is one that multicultural proponents and opponents will struggle over forever. Former impeached U.S.A. Vice President Spiro Agnew discovered the lesson is racism by his comment, "One Jap is like another Jap," so one needs to speak with respect of different kinds of persons. Henri J. M. Nouwan says, "Too often our words are superfluous, unauthentic and shallow," as he calls for silence instead of words (Nouwan, H. J. M., 1981).

Pope John Paul II has written in a recently published article in the *New York Times* containing the following insights on why we have so many religions in the world:

> Thus, instead of marveling at the fact that Providence allows such a great variety of religions, we should be amazed at the number of common elements found within them . . . The indigenous peoples of Australia boast a history of tens of thousands of years old, and their ethnic and religious tradition is older than that of Abraham and Moses.
>
> Pope John Paul II, 1994

With regard to the Pope's recognition of multiculturalism, he wrote of how some world religions have systems of worship and ethical principles with a strong emphasis on good and evil. He wrote:

> Certainly among these belong Chinese Confucianism and Taoism. Tao means eternal truth—which is reflected in the action of man to means of truth and moral good.
>
> Pope John Paul II, 1994

Mohandas Gandhi also supported this idea of Pope John Paul II as he claimed certain fundamental religious values were common to Judaism, Christianity, Buddhism and Hinduism such as a search for truth and non-violence. What the Pope and Gandhi mentioned here does not detract from the unique position of each religion, but it opens the door for dialog so humans might learn to live in harmony and peace on this planet.

American higher education has, in the past ten years, been dealt some problems to present college students such as:

1. The federal government has shifted the federal scholarships for the needy to more loans so students graduate with higher debts than ever before in history. Ethnic minorities, who have had little or no funds to attend college, have been hurt even more than ever in our country as their Pell Grants were reduced.
2. States are decreasing funds for higher education so proportionally short changing college students across our country so that less money than ever before in history is available for public higher education on a prorated basis.
3. Another serious problem in the 1980's and 1990's for the college student is that few, if any, summer jobs have existed that can be used to pay the entire year's cost of college.
4. In graduate school, some assistantships have been cut and their stipends have not been raised for years. Thus, stipends are very low and inadequate for many graduate students.

Finally, American college students have, in the 1990's, had difficulty getting jobs suitable for a four-year college graduate. To make matters worse, they have taken USA minimum wage jobs, done volunteer work, traveled abroad to work, and gone on to graduate and professional schools to fill in the time normally that might have been a job.

Telling the Truth

If higher education is to teach skills of critical thinking and analyzing subjects, how can a scholar avoid being judgmental or critical of a topic (weakness and strengths of a subject). We should tell the truth of each culture's immoral behavior from the fact that the Aztecs of Central America, in the 15th Century, practiced human sacrifice of their people to some units of the U.S. Cavalry who practiced genocide against the Navaho Indians in the 19th Century in Southwest America.

Howard Nash and his colleagues who composed the 1994 guide, *The 31 Standards for Teaching U.S. History,* has some shortcomings from not mentioning the U.S. Constitution in the Standards to neglecting Orville and Wilbur Wright and Thomas Edison as Chief inventors in history. While Nash and associates mention Eli Whitney's invention of the cotton gin and George Washington Carver's peanut research, the inventors of the airplane and electricity were forgotten Americans. Also, Nash and his scholars failed to mention that the U.S.A. has more ethnic minorities living peacefully together than any nation in the world up to this time. We need more than the political history of social history. It's culture that sets us apart and language links us with culture. When scholars use the "value free," "values neutral" and "cultural relative" approaches only and not present all the theories of culture, they are not offering students an objective approach to higher education.

References

Bennet, C. I. (1995). *Comprehensive multicultural education.* Boston, Massachusetts: Allyn and Bacon.

Davenport, D. S. and Yurich, J. M. (1991). Multicultural gender issues. *Journal of Counseling and Development, 70,* 64-71.

Eddy, J. P. (1995). *International Higher Education Systems.* Denton, Texas: RonJon Publishers.

———. *The NEA 1995 Almanac of Higher Education.* Washington, D.C.: National Education Association.

Eddy, J. P. (1994). International higher education research. Austin, Texas: Refereed professional paper presented at the annual conference of the Texas College and University Student Personnel Administrators.

Eddy, J. P. (1977). *College student personnel development, administration and counseling.* Washington, D.C.: University Press of America.

Fulcuyama, M. A. (1990). Taking a universal approach to multicultural counseling. *Counselor Education and Supervision, 30,* 6-17.

Gollnick, D. M. (1994). Focus on performance. *NCATE Newsletter,* 6-7.

Green, S. I. C. and Bobele, M. (1994). Family therapists' response to AIDS: An examination of attitudes, knowledge, and contact. *Journal of Marital and Family Therapy, 10*(4), 349-367.

Groth-Marnat, G. (1990). *Handbook of psychological assessment.* (2nd ed.). New York, New York: Wiley.

The Nation's Students. (1992, August 26). *The Chronicle of Higher Education,* 9-11.

National Association of Student Personnel Administrators 1993-94 Annual Report. (1994). Washington, D.C.: Nation Association of Student Personnel Administrators Publishers.

Nouwan, J. J. M. (1981). *The way of the heart.* San Francisco, California: Harper Publishers, 65.

Pederson, P. (1988). *A handbook for developing multicultural awareness.* Alexandria, Virginia: American Association for Counseling and Development.

Pope John Paul II. (1994, October 17). Why so many religions? *New York Times,* page A36.

Pleck, J.; O'Donnel, L.; O'Donnel, C.; and Snarey, J. (1988). AIDS-Phobia, contact with AIDS, and AIDS-related job stress in hospital workers. *Journal of Homosexuality.* 15, 41-54.

Prediger, D. J. (1993). *Multicultural assessment standards: A compilation for counselors.* Alexandria, Virginia: Association for Assessment in Counseling.

Serow, R. C.(1994). *Social foundations of American education.* Durham, North Carolina: Carolina Academic Press.

Sternberg, R. V. (1986). What would better intelligence tests look like? *Measures in the college admission process.* (Pp. 146-150). New York, New York: The College Entrance Examination Board.

Sue, D. W. and Sue, D. (1990). *Counseling the culturally different: Theory and practice.* New York, New York: Wiley.

Tracey, T. J. and Sedlacek, W. E. (1987). Prediction of college graduation using noncognitive variables by race. *Measurement and evaluation in counseling and development,* 19, 177-184.

Chapter 12

ಬಂಚ

Conflict Resolution Education Needed

Introduction

Over 6,000 religious leaders from around the world met in the Palmer House Hotel in Chicago, Illinois, USA in September, 1993 to discuss ways to allow their religious groups to resolve conflicts and not be used to justify conflict between peoples worldwide. Having attended, over the years, many conferences in the Palmer House Hotel, this conference made real sense. In a world of many diverse religious groups of which some religious leaders use religion for their own political agenda or personal power while ignoring the very basics of their religion's principles, this conference was an essential one to hold (Geyer, 1993).

Declaration of a Global Ethic

One of the highlights of the conference was the signing of a "Declaration of a global ethic Statement" by some of the conference goers. This statement was drafted to be a religious counter-ethic to conflict in a world where religion is still misused by leaders for political and personal gains. The statement that is nine pages in length contains some very powerful rhetoric such as the following:

We affirm that a common set of core values is found in the teachings of religions and that these form the basis of a global ethic . . . Rights without morality cannot long endure and that there will be no better global order without global ethic . . . This means a fundamental consensus on binding values, irrevocable standards and personal attitudes. (Excerpts from the "Declaration of a Global Ethic," 1993).

Conflict Resolution Sessions

Another important emphasis of the conference were helpful sessions on conflict resolution techniques instead of the conflict encouragement methods often used by some religious leaders to guide their converts into conflicts, battles and wars. The authors have used such conflict resolution techniques in their classes and in workshops overseas. One of the best conflict resolution approaches is included in Table 11.1.

Techniques for Arriving at Consensus

Fisher and Ury (1982) have written as follows:

Separate the people from the problem. Positional bargaining puts relationships and substance in conflict. Separate the relationship from the substances deal directly with the people problem. Consider their side of the issues and the way they perceive the problem. Recognize, understand, and make allowances for emotions, theirs and yours. Listen actively and acknowledge what is being said. Speak only for a purpose.

Focus on interests, not positions. For a wise solution reconcile interests, not positions. Behind opposing positions lie shared and compatible interests, as well as conflicting ones. Identify both, make a list, and talk about interests. Be hard on the problem, soft on the people.

Invent options for mutual gain. Beware of assuming that there is a single answer or a fixed pie. Recognize that both sides must act to solve the problem. Separate inventing from deciding. Consider brainstorming with the other side. Broaden your options. Look for mutual gain. Make their decisions easy.

Insist on objective criteria. By using objective criteria, principled negotiation produces wise agreements amicably and efficiently. Consider fair standards and procedures to determine objective criteria. When negotiating with objective criteria, reason and be open to reason. Never yield to pressure.

Table 11.1

Negotiation Strategies For Administrators, Counselors, Teachers, and Others: From Personal Relationships To International Conflicts

An applicable method for resolving conflicts
on all levels through problem solving

Soft	Hard	Principled
Participants are friends. The goal is agreement.	Participants are adversaries. The goal is victory.	Participants are problem solvers. The goal is a wise outcome reached efficiently and amicably.
Make concessions to cultivate the relationship.	Demand concessions as a condition of the relationship.	Separate the people from the problem.
Be soft on the people and the problem. Trust others.	Be hard on the problem and the people. Distrust others.	Be soft on the people and hard on the problem. Proceed independent of trust.
Change your position easily. Make offers. Disclose your bottom line.	Dig into your position. Make threats. Mislead as to your bottom line.	Focus interests, not positions. Explore interests. Avoid having a bottom line.
Accept one-sided losses to reach agreement. Search for the single answer: the one they will accept.	Demand one-sided gains as the price of agreement. Search for the single answer: the one you will accept.	Invent options of mutual gain. Develop multiple options to choose from; decide later.
Insist on agreement. Try to avoid a contest of wills.	Insist on your position. Try to win a contest of will.	Insist on using objective criteria. Try to reach a result based on standards independent of will.
Yield to pressure.	Apply pressure.	Reason and be open to reason; yield to principle.

Provided by Fisher and Ury, 1982, in their book.

Conclusion

Dr. Narithookil Xavier—Indian-born psychiatrist who practices in Birmingham, Alabama—said this about the conference: "What is happening here is that we are going beyond dogma to ethics . . . so to communicate." (Geyers 1993).

References

Eddy, J. P. (1993). Conflict resolution education. Denton, Texas: Unpublished paper delivered at the University of North Texas, September 23.

Fisher, R. and Ury, W. (1982). *Getting to yes: Negotiating agreement without giving in.* New York: Penguin Books.

Geyer, G. A. (1993). Principles to resolve conflicts. *Denton Record-Chronicle.* September 9, 6A.

Geyer, G. A. (1993). Few protestants at parliament. *Denton Record-Chronicle.* September 11, 6A.

Chapter 13

ℰᎧℭℛ

Building Community in College Classes

Introduction

C ollege classes offer an opportunity to build "community" in American society. What do the authors mean by "community"? "Community" is that attitude on the part of citizens to be responsible for each other, to care for each other and to be tolerant of each other. "Community" is coming over to a needy person's home to help your neighbor in a troubled time. "Community" is stopping your vehicle to aid a stranded person along the highway—the Good Samaritan Story in 1994. "Community" is dropping a family celebration for an hour to fix up a neighbor's house that has been damaged. What do these "community" examples here remind one of in America's many cultures? It reminds the lead author of a small town in Minnesota where I was born and grew up: A Garrison Keillor of Lake Wobegon village created out of the "Prairie Home Companion National Public Radio Series" in St. Paul, Minnesota.

It is fashionable to go and reminisce of the glorious past in agricultural rural America. That kind of "community" was and still is a fine model of persons caring for each other. However, in a city culture how can we begin to recapture "community" in our homes in cities that are like fortresses protecting our environment from our neighbors by fences, walls, security systems, barred windows, heavy metal doors, and attack dogs. Isolation, fragmentation and alienation face so many today so the value of "directed dyads" to build community is essential.

The College is a Place to Begin

The college or university is a place to teach "community" today. Every college has hundreds and even thousands of chances to do this in each and every college class. In America, 14 million college students could learn each year how to be "community members." These newly educated "community members" could take their knowledge of being a "community catalyst" back to their neighbors and start a "community revival, reformation and restoration" of America. Of course, human behavior changes are dependent on cooperative participants and facilitative persons who can work together effectively.

The Dynamic Dyad Can Make "Community"

In our college classes, we divide up our classes into pairs of two students called dyads (Nwafor and Eddy, 1993). These partners of students work together each university academic term to build "community" with each other, their fellow classmates and the professor. What have been the research results with over 400 students in a six year study? Here are some results:

1. Students learn to care for each other from helping a disability accommodation student take notes to aiding a student who was absent from class to catch up on missed lessons.
2. Students plan ways to make the course more vital and valuable because they have a mechanisms to give feedback to their professor who is not defensive but facilitative on their suggestions.
3. Students make their environment better by forming a food committee and a room accommodations committee in long classes that go, three, four and eight hours in length in one day.
4. Student work on personal health goals and academic goals in these dyads so they can take pride in their accomplishing objectives that may save their life like stopping smoking to

improving their career opportunities like preparing a professional journal article.

Self-Directed Work Teams

This is the age of self-directed work teams. These are small groups of employees, students or volunteers of an organization who have a particular design plan to attempt to work together on specific projects. The dynamic dyad (Eddy, 1994) is such a self-directed work team. This dyad can be done in all kinds of units of society such as family, religious bodies, voluntary organizations, school or college classes, governmental agencies, business, industries, military forces, or whatever persons gather to work, act or play (Murphy and Eddy, 1995; Murphy, Eddy and Spaulding, 1997).

Long Range Behavioral Changes

Some examples of dyad long range person behavioral change are the following:

1. S.K.L. quit cigarette smoking in 1988, and in 1994 he is still smoke free from a personal report in July, 1994.
2. U.M. decided to write articles for publication in 1988, and in 1994 he still is writing articles from a personal report in July, 1994.
3. C.V. made up his mind to improve his writing abilities in 1988, and in 1994 he still is improving his writing from a personal report in July, 1994.
4. D.M. committed himself in 1988 to get a statewide research project completed and published in a refereed journal, and in 1994 he accomplished this goal from a personal report in July, 1994.
5. J.E. vowed to write funded grants in 1988 and in 1994 he is still getting grants funded in 1994 from a personal report in July, 1994.
6. R.O. stopped his alcohol drinking problem in 1988, and in 1994 is still dry from a personal report in July, 1994.
7. Eight students in a course using dyads in 1992 reported by 1994 grants totaling over $700,000, inspired by dyad work.

A Ph.D. Doesn't Make One Cooperative
DR. JOHN PAUL EDDY

Having a Ph.D. alone doesn't improve one's ability to work in a self-directed work team. Persons with Ph.Ds, who should know better, can be as offensive and destructive on self-directed work teams as any person. I recall a government grant I was involved with in systems engineering many years ago whose objective was to have small groups effectively accomplish a task of writing a manual in two months. The first thing we had to do was to break down the problems of individualism, competition, status, and power seekers that get in the way of accomplishing goals in group work. Some persons have unwillingness to work with other persons and will even sabotage a project to avoid cooperation. The British file, "Oxford Blues" is a good example of such behavior of an American student at Oxford University who wouldn't cooperate with his rowing team.

Opportunities for Dyads in the Classroom

1. Dyads can improve human relationships between students and professors (Eddy, 1994).
2. Dyads can help set life long goals that will continue well beyond the course (Eddy, 1994).
3. Dyads can help improve a person's lifestyle, health and a students academic performance (Eddy, 1994).
4. Dyads can personalize a depersonalized classroom (Eddy, 1994).
5. Dyads can decrease student attrition and increase student retention (Eddy, 1994).
6. Dyads can provide a network for student support (Eddy, 1994).
7. Dyads provide a network for student support (Eddy, 1994).
8. Dyads can offer a team to do certain class projects (Eddy, 1994).
9. Dyads can help students better understand differences in a person's culture and background (Eddy, 1994).
10. Dyads can assist students in developing their graduate work and their career experiences (Eddy, 1994).

11. Dyads can help improve a person's self-esteem (Eddy, 1994).
12. Dyads can encourage a person to be more caring for another person (Eddy, 1994).

Conclusion

This presentation on research on dyads (Eddy, 1993) from 1988 to 1994 presents six years of evidence on how the behavior of students was changed. The effectiveness of dyad activity, for some persons, seems long lasting. The behavioral change may not be reinforced by dyad work for years, yet the original dyad work still keeps the person doing his goal going. Drucker, 1994, believes the self-directed work team is the key for unity, community and productivity of persons in the work force.

Bellah and Adams, 1994, writes that specialization in our urban culture removes "community" from life because it promotes a plurality of individual worlds and dissolves continuity among persons as common concerns are missing. Ironically, colleges are centers of specialization with various disciplines in America. These very institutions of higher education can now be centers for a "community development" via the dyad approach advocated here by the authors because dyads can build "community." In April, 1994 the lead author asked Dr. Robert Bellah at Austin College in Sherman, Texas a question on creating "community" in our culture, and his answer was that we should as Americans keep our volunteer organizations strong to help accomplish this task.

The dyad system of Eddy (Eddy, 1993) is one of the first college student development theories to have research evidence of its success. The dyad systems is based on "The Eddy Wholistic Model of College and Student Development" (Martin, Eddy, and Stilson, 1983: Murphy and Eddy, 1995; Murphy, Eddy and Spaulding, 1997). Dyads have proven to be a "bonding agent" for many students.

References

Bellah, R. N. and Adams, C. F. (1994). *Strong institutions, good city. Christian Century.* 3, (19), 604-607.

Drucker, P. F. (1994). The age of social transformation. *Atlantic Monthly,* 274 (5), 53-80.

Eddy, J. P. (1993). *Higher Education perspectives for leaders.* Edina, Minnesota: Burgess International Group Publishing, 93-109.

Eddy, J. P. (1994). Six year research study on dyad participants in university courses. Denton, Texas: Unpublished manuscript presented in EDHE 6730 on July 19, 1994.

Martin, B. E.; Eddy, J. P.; and Stilson, D. C. (1993). *Human development education: Principles, plans and problems.* Minneapolis, Minnesota: Burgess Publishing Company.

Murphy, S. and Eddy, J. P. (1995). The use of the dyad concept in residence hall student development. *College Student Journal* 29(1), 53-56.

Murphy, S. D.; Eddy, J. P.; and Spauling, D. J. (1997). College Residence Halls Research Study: Student perceptions of resident assistants, fellow residents, and residence hall living. *College Student Journal,* 31 (1), 110-114.

Nwafor, S. and Eddy, J. P. (1003). Dyad: An empirical examination of a dyad process to higher education courses. *College Student Journal.* 27 (2), 231-233.

Ngwokaegbe, P. U. (1991). The theoretical background for the dyad process of John Paul Eddy. Denton, Texas: Unpublished doctoral special problems paper at the University of North Texas, 1-6.

Chapter 14

℘ℂ℞

Factors in Problem-Solving Skills and Decision-Making Abilities: Applying History and Philosophy in Higher Education Abroad

Introduction

Billy Mitchell had outstanding ability to see future air power needs, future enemies, future airplane development and future airplane strategies in future wars. However, General Mitchell lacked "people skills" in dealing with his fellow military leaders and his reports lacked facts that could be supported by other authorities. Thus, his "problem solving skills" were limited by his research work shortcomings.

Much can be learned from the Billy Mitchell story. Here was a General who supported the start of the Air Force Academy in American higher education. He was an eager student who went back to school to retrain himself again and again for more modern military practices.

Some of the lessons learned from the Billy Mitchell story are provided here in summary. This is another case study on decision making skills.

1. **Problem solving skills and decision making abilities** are described here as strategies to apply appropriate ideas to resolve problems in higher education.

2. **Knowledge of history and philosophy** is the key to having the information to develop problem solving and decision making abilities. However, with history there is the difficulty of textbooks that do not present all the relevant facts about events and people so an accurate picture is often missing. Again, with philosophy there are so many schools of philosophy so persons have to pick and choose what schools they identify with. Having more **depth** of historical coverage or **breadth** of philosophical content is not the total answer because historians say the study of history and philosophers is not enough. It is not what key leaders and decision makers know but it is what they do with the knowledge they have to resolve problems.

3. **Case studies analysis** is a technique or method whereby problem solving skills are identified and applied so higher education personnel—administrators, faculty and counselors—can use their best decision making abilities to resolve problems in colleges and universities. **Using the scientific method**, as a schema for case studies analysis, students can maximize their learning experiences.

4. **Directed dyads—self-directed work teams**—provide an excellent opportunity for students to work on case studies analysis using the scientific method. Two students working one on one have the maximum chance to use the process of identifying the problem, finding alternative possibilities to resolve the problem, applying one or more of the alternatives to resolve the problem and evaluating how well the problem is resolved.

5. **An important factor** in decision making is the rhetoric decision makers use in stating their position. For example, General Mitchell used these words to describe his superiors in the U.S. Army and U.S. Navy with regard to the use of military air power and the accidents of our plans: "These accidents are the direct result of incompetence, criminal negligence and almost treasonable administration of the national defense by the War and Navy Departments." [Davis,

B. (1967). *The Billy Mitchell Affair*. New York, New York: Random House, p. 285.] This statement was the key sentence that caused his military court-martial under the 96th Article of War. This statement was "insubordinate . . . to the prejudice of good order and military discipline" and was "highly contemptuous and disrespectful" (Davis, 1976, p. 247).

The problem was that Mitchell fought for his ideas while still in the military, and he went to the media or they went to him so the affair was in national headlines. Also, some of his friends indicated he tended to over exaggerate and overstate his case. Thus, his decision making capacities for resolutions were handicapped by this behavior. Moreover, he seemed to use the court-martial itself to make his case which seemed illogical and years later he regretted this approach to S.L.A. Marshall (Davis, 1967, p 249).

6. **Giving an example** of how this all comes together in learning. (See Table 14.1.)

7. **The knowledge of history and philosophy** is essential in higher education but the ability of a person to know the environment by sociological analysis and to control one's behavior (psychological self insights) in a particular setting takes one's problem solving skills and decision making abilities into full account. Thus, it is seen that historical, philosophical, sociological, and psychological information is as vital as this course has mentioned. (See Table 14.2.)

Table 14.1

Historical Event	Philosophical Position	What Went Wrong in America?
Pearl Harbor, Hawaii December 7, 1941 had 3,581 casualties and the U.S. Navy had 18 ships destroyed as well as 174 airplanes in the area lost. Pearl Harbor has become the theme of every American who wants to protect his or her country from foreign harm.	General Billy Mitchell predicted that the attack would come by the Japanese airplanes in 1922 because Japan's philosophical position was then that America was the enemy blocking her (Japan's) dominance in Asia and had to be eventually dealt with. Mitchell changed his own philosophical positions on air power in 1917, and it showed our experiences in activity, such as John Dewey promoted, can change a person's philosophy.	The U.S. government's leaders ignored the historical information of General Billy Mitchell's prediction and his suggestions to defend Hawaii and Japan's philosophy outlined by General Mitchell. How could so many intelligent Americans be so incapable to deal with Japan in the Pacific region for nearly twenty years? This is a classic case of how America's best leaders ignored history and philosophy. Also, the lack of case studies analysis and the scientific method is apparent to resolve an international crisis. However, Mitchell held ideas like his superior until World War I when he experienced how air power can change the course of a battle. From that time on, he was a strong advocate, and if anyone opposed his views, he argued strongly against them. However, in defense of his opponents, the nation did not provide resources for Mitchell's views so this was a key problem.

Table 14.2

Sociological Observations	Psychological Observations
1. Sociological observations of the Billy Mitchell era verified some of the following:	1. Psychological observations of Billy Mitchell's personality by his critics included some of these insights:
A. The public tended to be isolationist by not supporting the League of Nations and not wanting to be involved the conflicts Japan and Germany were in before World War II. B. The public did not support U.S. military buildups in the 1920s or 1930s as the American economic depression from 1932 to 1941 kept the public preoccupied with self survival and not as interested in military causes as important as they were then and later.	A. Mitchell had "remarkable gifts and unusual energy in trying to alert his countrymen to the promise of aviation" but his "relentless insistence on the correctness of his beliefs ultimately destroyed him" (Hurley, a. F. (1975). Billy Mitchell: Crusader for Air Power. Bloomington, Indiana: Indiana University Press, page 140.). B. Mitchell underestimated the seriousness of the court-martial proceedings according to Mrs. Hap Arnold whose husband was once the U.S. Air Force Chief General (Davis, 1967, page 253). C. According to Secretary of War Weeks, "General Mitchell sometimes talks indiscreetly" (Davis, 1967, page 203).

Chapter 15

ಐಂಣ

Conclusion

DR. JOHN PAUL EDDY

This reference book has offered a modest potpourri of topics in its chapters that have selectively covered the field of international education as it relates to higher education in the United States of America and to over 40 countries of the world (Eddy, Spaulding and Maronga, 1994). The reference volume has provided valuable resources and information for students of higher education to use in their research, publishing, grants procurement, teaching, overseas travel, service, advisement, counseling, administration referrals and professional groups (Eddy, 1994).

Important current research studies, appearing in refereed journals, are given in an annotated style to aid the reader in finding these resources for their additional study and utilization (Eddy, 1993). Helpful information and insights on higher education subjects in other nations are carefully identified and briefly described for further scholarly investigation (Hazajneh and Eddy, 1994). The intent of this reference work was not to be encyclopedic but to be hopefully relevant for those looking deeper into international higher education elements of conflict, challenge, crescendo, crisis, concern and cooperation to build a better world.

Perhaps the wise wisdom of the renown Dutch scholar, Dr. Henri J. M. Nouwen, who once taught at Yale University and has lectured widely across the world, is noteworthy to quote here on how one person can only do so much on this planet:

> I think newspapers are very seductive things—they surround us with the misery of the world without our being able to do anything about it. We have to do what we are called to do. . . . (Graham, 1994).

Again, the world needs persons who change conditions that imprison persons in racism, employment and hunger. Nouwen addresses this mentioning some persons I have met:

> If you think of all the prophets in our modern times—Martin Luther King, Jr., Cesar Chavez, or Dorothy Day—they are people who began by doing small things. I'm talking about small in the sense that what they did, did not change everything overnight. They opened a soup kitchen or work for the migrant workers or labored for the liberation of the black people. . . . (Graham, 1994).

In this book, the authors mentioned the importance of values like never giving up and traveling abroad to gain new ideas. In the book, *Schindler's Legacy,* the story of Oskar Schindler and the Holocaust is told by thirty individuals' stories of survival from the Nazi German genocide who came to make America their new homeland. The stories have a strange mix of what these successful survivors did in America since their prison camp hell with flash backs of what they suffered from in the horror of the camps. One sentence struck me as particularly evil as the Nazis forced Jewish prisoners in Poland to do the following: "Prisoners grabbed the dead bodies of prisoners—and pitched them into a mass grave . . . all day and into the night, without stopping" (Brecher, 1994).

Another illustration of never giving up, is seen in the book, *The Delany Sisters'.* In the summer of 1994, we had the chance to interview Professor Julian Bond, Professor of American Civil Rights History at American University in Washington, D.C. Professor bond, who worked with Dr. Martin Luther King, Jr. on civil rights leadership in America, calls the Delany Sisters a national treasure. These two African American women, Sarah (a school teacher) and A. Espalier (a dentist), now 105 and 103 years old, have written a book, published by a Japanese publisher, that has outstanding wisdom because they have never given up on life. Some ideas are: (1) When you want to keep young, you exercise regardless of your feeling against exercise. (2) When you are not educated, you lose control of your life. (3) When you have spiritual faith, you are prepared for life and can do something with your life. (4) When it comes to daily eating, we eat seven different vegetables and good breakfast of oatmeal, eggs, fruit and a hard roll. (5) When it comes to daily helping people, we tutor school children after school so they will not be alone with their parents working. (6) When it comes to interracial relationships, we are proud of who we are — part white and part Negro. (7) When it comes to handling our garbage, we reuse and recycle all we can. (8) When it comes to our conscience, a sense of right and wrong is essential in life. (9) When it comes to television — it can educate or entertain — but it can also rot a person's brain instead of reading, thinking or doing. (10) When it comes to who is a great person, it is how the persons treats his or her spouse and children and other persons that makes a great person. These sages of the ages are examples of good role modeling across the world for persons in all cultures. The authors would include them, in their lectures delivered in the first credit course in Women's Studies at the University of North Texas in the Spring semester of 1994, as minority role models representing the United States of America as African American women of highest achievement. These women are examples of life long learning and of putting their values to work in making this a better world—that is what we need to teach and practice in higher education institutions across the world as well as in all positions of employment everywhere.

One needs a positive and peaceful philosophy of life to work for a better world. In 1994, Palestinians and the Israelis shook hands on the United States White House lawn. The citizens of the Union of South Africa elected a rainbow government throwing off the racial barrier of apartheid and putting into leadership a Black leader who once was in prison for 26 years for his political views. Miracles these two events are and miracles are what makes a better world especially when we work for miracles of freedom, equality, harmony and peace among all peoples.

References

Brecher, E. J. (1994). *Schindler's Legacy: True stories of the list survivors.* New York, New York: Penguin Books.

Delany, S. and Delany, A. E. (1994). *The Delany sisters': book of everyday wisdom.* New York, New York: Kodansha International Publishers.

Eddy, J. P. (April, 1994). Minority issues in professional counseling organizations. Minneapolis, Minnesota: American Mental Health Counselors Association National Conference.

Eddy, J. P.; Spaulding, D. and Maronga, G. B. (March, 1994). Deans of students national research assessment: Kenya and China studies. Indianapolis, Indiana: American College Personnel Association National convention.

Eddy, J. P. (1993). Using Deming to improve quality in colleges and universities by Comesby, R. and et al. Madison, Wisconsin: Magna Publications, Inc., 1992, reviewed in *Journal of Staff Program and Organization,* 11 (2), 59-60.

Graham, G. R. (November/December, 1994). Interview with Henri Nouwen. *Alice Now,* 36-43.

Hayaineh, A. and Eddy, J. (April, 1994). Values of middle east college graduates as executives. Minneapolis, Minnesota: American Association for Wellness, Counseling and Research National Conference.

Appendix A

ᏍᎧ

International Education Administrative Office

Dr. Tom Barker and Dr. John Eddy

A survey of the literature reveals that few students in the international student office exist such as Rice-Maximin and Zafar in Eddy, 1995. Nevertheless, Aigner, Nelson and Stimpfl (1992) find administration as one of the areas in operationalizing the process to internationalize universities. The need for strong support for international education has been recognized by Adams (1979), Arum (1987), Lambert (1989), Pickert and Turlington (1992), Posvar (1980), and Smuclaler and Sommers (1988). These authors did not specifically address how the support was (or should be) manifested on campus.

Suggestions about administrative office are given by Adams (1979), good (1977), Kellerher (1991), and Pickert (1992). Davies (1992) suggested that the delivery of international services could be either through normal organizational units or a special organ developed for the purpose. Arum (1987) presented ideas on both a centralized and a diffusionist strategy. He presented an argument for the latter because of the involvement of many elements of the institution. A counter argument that favors a centralist strategy is an international office on campus gives international education a high profile on campus, it serves as a focal point for international education programs and activities, and it gives the administration a measure of control not possible with a diffusionist strategy. Michie (1970) found that many higher education institutions had institutionalized international education with a new campus structure, the international office. This article examines the international education administrative offices in Texas colleges and universities to determine which are the strategies that have been followed in the state. Fifty-six of the seventy-nine Texas four-year institutions responded to the survey.

Methodology

A review of the literature did not disclose a suitable questionnaire to explore this area. A survey instrument was developed that included questions about the international education office.

Instrument

The instrument, Survey of International Education Programs in the State of Texas, was developed. Validity was established using a panel of experts who are nationally known for their expertise in international education. Reliability was established by having selected personnel in international offices in state colleges and universities complete the survey form. Their responses were compared to the returns from the instrument that was mailed to presidents/chancellors of the same institutions.

Data Analysis

Data was computed based on the affirmative responses to the questions and the number of institutions responding to each question. Tables A.1 and A.2 reflect the results.

Approximately half of the Texas institutions had an international education office. Twenty-six institutions provided names of the administrative office; 37.5% of the institutions surveyed reported an office with International in the title; 10.10% reported an office without International in the title. The other either did not have an office or did not report the name. Forty-one institutions responded to a question about the head of the international office. Forty-six and four tenths of the institutions reported that the head was a director or coordinator;

Table A.1
International Education Administrative Office

Institution	Number of responses and % yes			
	Public #	Private #	Medical #	Total #
International education administrative office	25 (56.0)	26 (46.20	2 (50.0)	53 (50.9)

5.4% were deans; 19.6% had other titles including one president, one associate vice-president and one associate vice chancellor. Table A.2 shows the campus official to which the head of the international office reports.

Forty-six institutions responded. In most cases (39.1%) the person in charge of the office reported to the vice president for academic affairs; however, 77.5% of the office administrators reported to the president, provost, or someone in academic affairs. The remainder reported to someone without direct involvement with academic affairs. It is noted that only 9.0% report to the vice president of student affairs. Based on these results, it is apparent that the offices have an academic orientation.

Conclusions

The findings of the survey permit some conclusions to be drawn concerning the international office on campuses of Texas four-year institutions.

1. Approximately half of the institutions had an international education office.
2. Of the Texas institutions with an international education office, 37.5% reported using the word international in the name of the office.
3. The person with primary responsibility for international education was a director or coordinator (46.4%), the others had various titles.
4. The person responsible for international education in most cases reported to the vice president for academic affairs. When considering the president, provost and others in academic affairs, the percentage is 77.5%.

Table A.2
Person Responsible for International Education Reports to:

Institution	Number of institutions and %			
	Public # %	**Private** # %	**Medical** # %	**Total** # %
President or Chancellor	1 (5.0)	2 (8.3)	1 (50.0)	4 (9.0)
Provost	4 (20.0)	1 (4.2)	0 (0.0)	5 (10.9)
Vice President— Academic Affairs	6 (30.0)	12 (50.0)	0 (0.0)	18 (39.1)
Vice President— Student Affairs	3 (15.0)	1 (4.2)	0 (0.0)	4 (9.0)
Other Vice President	0 (0.0)	4 (16.7)	0 (0.0)	4 (9.0)
Other, within Academic Affairs	2 (10.0)	2 (8.3)	0 (0.0)	4 (9.0)
Other, within Student Affairs	1 (5.0)	0 (0.0)	0 (0.0)	1 (2.2)
Other	3 (15.0)	2 (8.3)	1 (50.0)	6 (13.0)

Recommendations

Based on this survey of Texas institutions, the following recommendations are made:

1. When an institution recognizes international education as part of its mission, that an international education office be established.
2. International education office be recognized with word international in the name of the office to give the office a profile on campus.
3. An individual responsible for either directing or coordinating international education be designated and be provided with an adequate staff to carry out the responsibilities assigned to the individual and office.
4. The person heading the international education office report to an individual in the top administration of the campus to further give credence to the office and the programs and activities of the office.

References

Adams, H. (1979). A rationale for international education. *New Directions for community Colleges,* 7(2), 1-10.

Aigner, J. S. , Nelson, P., & Stimpfl, J. R. (1992). *Internationalizing the university: Making it work.* Lincoln, NE: University of Nebraska. (ERIC Document Reproduction Service NO. ED 342 316).

Arum, S. (1987). *International education: What is it? A taxonomy of international education of U.S. universities.* New York: council on International Exchange. (ERIC Document Reproduction Service No. ED 305 835).

Davies, J. L. (1992). Developing a strategy for internationalization in universities: Toward a conceptual framework. In C. B. Klasek (Ed.), *Bridges to the future: Strategies for internationalizing higher education* (pp. 177-189). Washington, DC: Association of International Educators.

Eddy, J. P. (1985). *International education and student development applications.* Edina, Minnesota: Burgess Publishing.

Good, R. C. (1977). The twenty-first century is now. *Educational Record.* 58(1), 18-30.

Kelleher, A. (1991). One world: Many voices. *Liberal Education,* 77(5), 2-7.

Lambert, R. D. (1989). *International studies and the undergraduate.* Washington, DC: American Council on Education.

Michie, A. A. (1970). Higher education and world affairs. In A. S. Knowles (Ed.), *Handbook for college and university administration general* (pp. 3-140 - 3163). New York: McGraw-Hill Book Company.

Pickert, S. M. (1992). *Preparing for a global community: Achieving an international perspective in higher education.* ASHE-ERIC Higher Education Report No. 2. Washington, DC: The George Washington University, School of Education and Human Development.

Pickert, S. M., & Turlington, B. (1992) *Internationalizing the curriculum: A handbook for campus leaders.* Washington, DC: American Council on Education.

Posvar, W. W. (1980). Toward an academic response: Expanding international dimensions. *Change,* 12(4), 23-26.

Smuckler, R., & Sommers, L. (1988). Internationalizing the curriculum: Higher education institutions in the United States. *National Forum: Phi Kappa Phi Journal,* 68(4), 5-10.

Appendix B

ଶୠ

Observations of Dr. W. Edwards Deming on Quality

The ideas of Dr. W. Edwards Deming, author of "Deming's Fourteen Points of Management," are provided here. This American scholar was first taken seriously in Japan before American business began to adopt his methods. Japanese industry leaders credited Deming with guiding them to success in world markets. Now, American Fortune 500 corporations use Deming's ideas in their team work efforts. This vividly illustrates the reason one needs to be involved in the study of what is going on in other nations and why the theme of this book is so important to higher education, governmental, business and other leaders worldwide. Again, the philosophy and practices of Dr. Deming provides approaches for all who use the "directed dyad"—a self-directed work team method— that is advocated in this volume for university credit courses as well as in work place settings.

Dr. Deming's Fourteen Points are summarized here as follows: (1) Create constancy of purpose; (2) Adopt the new philosophy; (3) Cease dependence on mass inspection to achieve quality; (4) End the practice of awarding business on price tag alone; (5) Improve constantly the system of production and service; (6) Institute training on the job; (7) Institute leadership; (8) Drive out fear; (9) Break down barriers between departments; (10) Eliminate slogans, exhortations, and numerical targets; (11) Eliminate work standards (quotas) and management by objectives; (12) Remove barriers that rob workers, engineers, and managers of their right to pride of workmanship; (13) Institute a vigorous program of education and self-improvement; and (14) Put everyone in the organization to work to accomplish the transformation. Thus Deming taught that better goods and services came from improvement of the quality of communications and relationships between managers, workers, customers and suppliers in the whole system loop of capitalism in a business.

References

Dobyns, Lloyd and Clare Crawford-Mason. (1994). *Thinking about quality: Progress, wisdom, and the Deming philosophy.* New York: Times Books.

Deming, W. Edwards. (1986). Out of the crisis, 2nd ed. Cambridge, MA: MIT Center for Advanced Engineering Study.

Deming, W. Edwards. (1993). *The new economics for industry, government, and education.* Cambridge, MA: MIT Center for Advanced Engineering Study.

Dobyns, Lloyd and Clare Crawford-Mason. (1991). *Quality or else: The revolution in world business.* Boston: Houghton-Mifflin.

Gitlow, Howard S. and Shelley J. (1987). *The Deming guide to quality and competitive position.* New Jersey: Prentice Hall, Inc.

Joiner, Brian L. (1994). *Fourth generation management, the new business consciousness.* New York: McGraw-Hill, Inc.

Neave, Henry. (1990). *The Deming dimension.* Knoxville, TN: SPC Press.

Scherkenbach, William W. (1986). *The Deming route to quality and productivity: Road maps and roadblocks.* Washington, D.C.: CeePress Books.

Scholtes, Peter et al. (1989). *The team handbook: How to use teams to improve quality.* Madison, WI: Joiner Associates.

Schultz, Louis E. (1994). *Profiles in quality, learning form the masters.* White Plains, New York: Quality Resources.

Walton, Mary. (1986). *The Deming management method.* New York: Dodd, Mead and Company.

Appendix C

୫୨୦୧୫

How to Develop
International Opportunities

W hat can we do to be more knowledgeable and understanding of persons from other countries across the world? There are many things we can do that will develop ourselves such as:

1. Communicating through Internet computer networks, FAX, phone and mail with scholars and officials in other lands;
2. Traveling to other nations to study their cultures, activities and peoples;
3. Inviting foreign citizens to our homes to discover their interests and data about their nations;
4. Reading about other nations' activities an culture;
5. Viewing informative films about other countries;
6. Simulating role playing experiences involving foreigners;
7. Listening to lectures on important matters in other countries;
8. Researching important materials on other nations in key books such as: *International Encyclopedia of Education, International Higher Education: An Encyclopedia, Handbook of World Education, Higher Education Cannot Escape*

History, Higher Education Perspectives for Leadership, The Academic Profession: An international Perspective, International Education and Student Development Applications, International Higher Education Systems, ASHE Reader on the History of Higher Education, World Education Encyclopedia, The World Almanac and Book of Facts 1995, World Guide to Education, Perspectives on World Education, International Bibliography of Comparative Education, World Guide to Higher Education: A comparative Survey of Systems, Degrees and Qualifications, World Education Encyclopedia, Current Issues in World Higher Education, Amnesty International Report 1994, International Academic Credentials Handbook, International Handbook of Universities, and others.

Appendix D

ℰᴑᴔ

Overseas: Living Through Difficult Experiences

DR. JOHN PAUL EDDY

In 1954, while working in an education mission in the Philippines, I experienced some very difficult problems that many people face daily in numerous developing nations across the globe such as:

1. Continuous wars between various tribal, ethnic, religious and national groups;
2. Deadly tropical diseases everywhere;
3. Shortage of food and safe drinking water;
4. Poisonous snakes and dangerous animals in the jungles;
5. Lack of law and order in the society; and
6. Inadequate medical, health, sanitation and social services.

Dr. Frank C. Laubach knew of these conditions that I have just mentioned for they come from Mindanao, Philippines where we both had work with the people there. Laubach, founder of the Laubach Literacy

Method which has taught hundreds of millions world-wide to read, has one of my votes for one of the greatest international educators who ever lived.   Laubach was a global role model as an international educator, missionary mystic, spiritual experimenter and leader among Christians world-wide.   I recall meeting him at the University of Kansas in Lawrence, Kansas and having a few minutes to talk to him.   Laubach once wrote in his classic book, *Letters by Modern Mystic,* page 54, these words that go beyond the rhetoric we hear about the international computer information highway today: "If we open both out draw bridges, we become God's highway." Laubach had that vision and that mission to help persons help themselves as in the "directed dyad program" advocated in my courses— his message was "each one teach one."   If we would give ourselves over to the ideas of Laubach on literacy we all would be a better world of people of purpose, of principle and of peace.

Appendix E

ℰℭ

A Cruel and Violent Century

T he need for peace education to be taught in our schools and colleges across the world is based on two observations by world-known authorities such as:

1. "This century of ours may well have been the cruelest and most violent in history, with its world and civil wars, its mass tortures, ethnic cleansing, genocides, and holo- causts . . . Hitler, Stalin and Mao, the three evil geniuses of this century, destroyed . . . but created nothing." [Drucker, P. F. (1994). The age of social transformation, *The Atlantic Monthly*, 274 *5, 53-80].

2. "After Nuremburg, it was generally anticipated by the international community that a new era had begun . . . but it was not to be. The past five decades have witnessed some of the gravest violations of humanitarian law" [Goldstone, R. (1994, November 8). War crimes tribunal opens. *Denton Record-Chronicle*, 91 (98), 1A-5A].

Comments on these statements are the following:

3. In 1984, the author had an opportunity to interview Dr. Peter F. Drucker, internationally known business management expert, so the above statements of Dr. Drucker are very revealing as he did not mention his views to me on how bad this century in history compared.

4. In 1974, the author began to work with Cambodians who suffered from a genocide by the communists that a book and a movie, "Killing Fields" presented. Thus, Prosecutor Richard Goldstone's statement on the Nuremberg and Tokyo War Crimes Courts, after World War II, is most revealing as this World Court Prosecutor has expressed an extremely negative result of these War Crimes trials changing the behavior of humans worldwide.

International Refugees

The international problem of refugees is a world crisis with more than 23 million people living in refugee-like situations according to the United Nations High Commissioner for Refugees (UNHCR). This is a large increase from the some 8 million at the end of the 1970s. In Africa alone, there are over 7.5 million refugees in 1995. (Ivey, D. C., 1995). "Refugees: A global perspective." New World Outlook, 50(3), 4-7.

Appendix F

ᔕᘐᣛ

A Historical Analysis of Dyads and Teamwork

Dr. John Paul Eddy

It is important to give an historical analysis of teamwork and dyads to point out it is an old concept for providing effective work. Jesus Christ over 2000 years ago asked his disciples to work in teams of two (dyads) as they covered Palestine. Military forces of nations around the world have used teams of two to do various scouting missions since the dawn of history. The team concept is not new, but it certainly is one some persons are still discovering after thousands of years of practice.

Peter Drucker has suggested the importance of teams and teamwork in organizations to improve motivation and production. Drucker has pointed out that this practice is not new but age old from the farmer and the farmer's wife who worked as a team. Again, the craftsman and his wife worked as a team as he did the craft work and she sold craft work. Again journeymen mentored apprentices so they worked as a team. Drucker wisely comments, "Much discussion today assumes that there is only one kind of team. Actually there are quite a few . . . so teams become the work unit rather than the individual himself." (Drucker, P. F. (1994). The age of social transformation. *The Atlantic Monthly,* 274 (5), 53-80.) Thus, Drucker is a strong supporter of the team approach (the dyad or small group) in making organizations effective and successful from businesses to universities for it is "the organization that performs."

Peace Building Groups

Peace building groups in such nations as Nicaragua, following the war there, are trying teamwork to teach opposing forces to live together without conflict or violence. Over 400 peace groups nationwide now exist there—91 in Nueva Guinea and 14 in the area of Jamilla [Wersan, S. (1995). "Building the peace in Central America." *New World Outlook,* 50(3), 27-29]. In Liberia, higher education institutions in 1995 are providing teaching on peace building according to reports from my doctoral students.

Appendix G

ℰℴℭℛ

Thoughts and Questions for Developing Leaders

DR. JOHN PAUL EDDY

S ome thoughts for developing 21st Century leaders as persons are the following:

1. "Our human nature is such that we need to be helpful, thoughtful and generous as much as we need to eat, sleep, and exercise. When we eat too much and exercise too little, we feel out of sorts." (Kushner, H. S. (1986). *When all you've ever wanted isn't enough.* New York, New York. Summit Books, pages 180-181).

2. "When one deals with the affairs of civilization, one is trying to make the principle of love effective as far as possible, but one cannot escape the conclusion that society as such is futile." (Niebuhr, R. (1980). *Leaves from the notebook of a tamed cynic.* Louisville, Kentucky: Westminster. John Knox Press, page 152).

3. "Leadership is not based on position but whether or not one is a servant. . . . The first concern must always be service to others, rather than worrying about exalting oneself . . . so there is more concern about the future than the past." (Blake, B. P. (1990). *A call to community, conviction and commitment.* Dallas, Texas. North Texas Conference of the United Methodist Church, page 8).

4. "My second son, whose back ripples with quick strength on a basketball court, is suddenly crippled by the mere mention of a lawn mower . . ." (Wangerin, W. (1993). *Little lamb who made thee.* Grand Rapids, Michigan: Zondervan Publishing House).

5. "In any case, there are many different ways of sharing the fruits of contemplation with others. . . . Prayer can do the work wonderfully well . . ." (Merton, T. (1985). *The seven story mountain.* New York, New York. Walker and Company, page 761).

6. "We have attempted to deny the human condition in our quest for power after power. It would be well for us to rejoin the human race, to accept our essential poverty as a gift, and to share our material wealth with those in need." (Bellah, R. N. and Association. (1985). *Habits of the heart.* Berkeley, California: University of California Press, page 296).

7. "If everyone in any kind of organization remembered that—results come when people are achieving what is important to them—there is no doubt in my mind that productivity, which seems to be such a serious problem in this country, would increase enormously, would soar. The manager who knows how to unblock, to free, to enhance the motivating forces in the people who report to him or her knows how to get performance results—superior performance results." (Quick, T. L. (1980). *The quick motivation method.* New York, New York. St. Martin's Press, page 191).

8. "Changing old patterns can be difficult if we operate with a mechanical or static model of reality and do not really believe that change is possible. But if we learn to read the signs of life all around us and we discover that we are indeed created to be creative, then we can rediscover the power and

resourcefulness of imagination—another aspect of the soul—so . . . we can change patterns we have grown up with and come home to our bodies as a source of wisdom." (Blankson, M. Z. (1993). *This is my body.* San Diego, California: Lura Media, pages 14-15).

9. "Emotions, especially excessive fear and anger, are always significant factors in personality. They are not simply mental experiences; they have far-reaching and violent physical reactions in the body itself. Faith cures have sound, physical bases." (Ligon, E. M. (1930). *Their future is now.* New York, New York. Macmillan Company, page 266).

10. "To love abundantly is to live abundantly, and to love forever is to live forever. Hence, eternal life is inextricably bound up with love." [Drumnlond, H. (1946). *The Greatest Thing in the World.* Carrnel, New York. Guideposts Associates, Inc., page 40].

11. "In 1963, I heard a lecture of Dr. Russell Kirk—former staff member of the Educational Research Council of America, recipient of the Presidential Citizens Medal, author of numerous books and articles on higher education—on one of his over 500 lectures to American educational institutions from 1951 to 1994.

Kirk wrote in his book, *The Conservative Mind,* that the number one problem facing us is "the problem of spiritual and moral regeneration: the restoration of the ethical system and the religious sanction upon which any life worth living is founded." [Kirk, Russell (1994). *The conservative mind: Burke to Eliot.* Bryn Maur, Pennsylvania: Intercollegiate Studies Institute.]

The Soviet writer Aleksandi Solzhenitsyn wrote, "Atheism is the core of the whole communist system . . . and if I were called upon to identify briefly the principal trait of the entire twentieth century, here too I would be unable to find anything more precise and pithy than to repeat once again: men have forgotten God . . . Every calamity of the century stems from the flow of a consciousness lacking all divine dimension." [Ericson, Edward E. (1994). Conservatism at it highest. *The intercollegiate Review.* 301,33.]

12. "The ancient Chinese, Egyptian, Greek and Roman civilizations all recognized that man is a tridimensional being. The spiritual aspect of man is the most important but the most neglected." [Ziglar, Zig. 91985). *Raising positive kids.* Nashville, Tennessee: Thomas Nelson Publishers, page 89.]

13. George Benson, educator in China—former long time President of Harding University of Searcy, Arkansas and founder of the National Education Program—at age 72 said: "When there are many decisions that have to be made over a period of years, you will make enemies, but you also make friends of fair minded people. I know I have made my share of enemies. I find I always had the majority of the faculty behind me. I did keep some whom I knew were very critical of me, but they did a good job for the college."

Appendix H

ଽଠ୯ଌ

Case Study: China

According to a 1995 Report of the Environmental Protection Agency, five of the ten most polluted cities of the world are in China. This illustrates how their government is allowing untreated fuel such as coal and not installing effective pollution devices on their factories, businesses, school and homes.

The modification of Communism to Capitalistic enterprises in China has led to many problems facing many developing nations as Farley, 1994, points out: "Like many emerging markets, China has its problems: few regulations, growing inflation, corruption and no role of law—investments have gone from $12 billion in 1991 to over $111 billion in 1993 . . . The results: Chinese companies are having problems paying creditors—domestic and foreign—and some resort to risky maneuvers to increase cash flow." (Farley, M. (1994, December, 29). "Latest China deals fragile." *Minneapolis Star Tribune,* page 1D and 4D.

Another sign of these changing times in Asia happened on January 5, 1995 when Taiwan—in a major foreign policy shift—lifted a ban on shipping with rival China so bringing these former long time enemies together in the export trade.

Why is Singapore's model being studied, with its free-market capitalism and strict rule, by other nations? Computer penetration in Singapore is among the greatest in the world. Why is China looking at the Singapore model?

Appendix I

ഔഐ

Case Studies: India, Iran, France and America

The excessive violence and sex shown on American television, that reaches audience across the world via satellites has caused reactions among some nation's people. For example, in Iran the government is banning American television programs entirely and in India some people are destroying their television sets entirely so they can't view the violent American television shows. The message of nonviolence by Mohandas K. Gandhi and Martin Luther King, Jr. were ahead of their time, and they refused to yield for what they believed. There is a strong message here for American media that long has neglected its role to govern, monitor, censor or restrict its violence in its film presentations. The freedom of speech excuse has been used to present the most evil and ugly violence on television in America.

Appendix J

ဇဝၥ

International Russia: What If?

DR. JOHN PAUL EDDY

What if the USA had never bought Alaska from Russia in 1867? The answer is that if it hadn't happened, Americans wouldn't have lived in Alaska since 1867. One of my friends has had homestead in Alaska for over 48 years. His adventures include many life and death experiences as can happen on a wilderness frontier and pioneering area. Some of these are included here as follows:

1. He was awakened by a friend in 50° below zero weather, or he would have frozen to death in a tent without adequate heat.
2. He was warned by forest rangers when a forest fire came through his farm burning up his trees.
3. He woke up to a fire burning in his cabin barely saving his life from smoke inhalation.
4. He chased a bear out of his cabin who could have killed him.
5. He dodged a charging moose who could have taken his life.

6. He drove his truck only a few feet from a flooded river that could have swept him to a watery death.

7. He exploded some old dangerous dynamite, that he underestimated its destruction power, that nearly took his life as his hill cave blew up.

8. He was driving a farm tractor cutting hay in his field when lightening struck his tractor and nearly killed him.

9. He was working for the North American Defense Command when snow storms and 70° below zero temperatures nearly cost him his life.

10. He survived the cooking of ten different vegetables raised on his Alaskan farm of 90 acres in an old fashioned pressure cooker by the author of this book in 1994.

This friend in Alaska has lived mostly on potatoes and other vegetables. The potato is one of the most valuable of vegetables for one can live off of it. The potato is an international story. Potatoes used in the U.S.A. have been developed over the last 300 years after being discovered in South America by way of Europe. For example, two varieties came to the U.S.A. by Spanish explorers who traded with Indian tribes on the West Coast, and one comes from the Tlingit Indian village on Prince of Wales Island off the Alaskan Coast. While in Alaska in August of 1994, I ate some of those potatoes as I also visited with some Tlingit Indians. In the TV series "Northern Exposure," these native Americans are also mentioned.

Appendix K

ℰℭ

Media Criticism Can
Impact World Affairs

DR. JOHN PAUL EDDY

1994 was the worst year in the worldwide media history for the loss of journalists. Over 130 journalists were killed mainly in Rwanda and Algeria by terrorist groups. Reporting conflicts and wars can be dangerous to one's health as some groups are against the freedom of the press giving the truthful reporting of events.

Sometimes words will challenge a person to change their life and help a human cause. Years ago Alfred Nobel, the Swedish chemist who invented dynamite, read in the newspaper that he had died. The obituary read that dynamite contributed a substance for war to take thousands of lives. Nobel was struck by this moral charge against his invention so he established the Nobel Peace Prize to honor those who worked for peace between people and nations. This started a worldwide concern for peacemaking because of a media mistake. [Moore, J. W. 1(1988). *Seizing the moments: Making the most of life's opportunities*. Nashville, Tennessee: Abingdon Press, page 19].

Appendix L

ဆ)ભ

The Progress of Communications Around the World

The 1995 Rose Bowl Parade in Pasadena, California was viewed by over 500,000,000 persons worldwide with bands and floats from Indonesia to China and Japan to illustrate how television can be a window to the entire world. Electronics developing in 1995 include such advancements as:

1. Interactive TV to provide information, movies, shopping and college credit courses at the customers' fingertips;
2. High Definition TV programming in North America;
3. CD size video disks containing full-length films;
4. 99 cent CD-ROM disks;
5. Satellite TV mini-disk systems for $399 or less;
6. Computer pens, run on a single battery, will send and receive data by an infrared beam;
7. Internet safeguards are having to be developed due to intruders who are using spoofing to steal information so both hardware and software fire walls are being installed for theft protection; and

8. Computer bulletin boards, suggesting how to make bombs, need to be removed from electronic mail banks by laws.

Appendix M

ℰ∂ℂℛ

Medical Miracles:
College Student Case Study

DR. JOHN PAUL EDDY

The medical miracles that exist today is illustrated in this true 1994 story of a college student at Wheaton College, Wheaton, Illinois. Years ago, when I left my position at Loyola University of Chicago, I donated my college Student Affairs Library to Wheaton College. On Eric's opposing teams are players from other nations such as Mexico and Canada to show how college sports have become internationalized in America. Of course, soccer is the number one sport in the world in terms of numbers of players and fans. Eric is a starting college soccer forward, who while playing against Trinity University in San Antonio, Texas, has heavy heart palpitations—170 beats per minute—so he had to quit playing. He had this condition since birth in 1974 but no doctor could find it. He was hospitalized in San Antonio and told he has Wolff-Parkinson White Syndrome. This is a condition that causes a fast heart rhythm when extra accessory pathways in the heart disrupt the normal electrical impulses of the heart. He returned to a Minneapolis, Minnesota hospital where he had a new surgical procedure at the Minnesota Heart Institute called radio frequency ablation that was so successful he returned to play college soccer to lead his team in scoring to the conference championship. The Wheaton College team qualified for its 20th post-season appearance in the NCAA Division III. From near sudden cardiac death without warning to a cure is a miracle.

Appendix N

ℰᏩᏓ

Hard to Understand International Conflicts

Some of the hard to understand international conflicts in foreign nations in 1994 include the following:

1. In Rwanda where one out of three persons suffers from AIDS, why would two tribes (the majority Hutu and the minority Tutsi tribes) kill over 500,000 persons causing the relocation of 2.5 million children, women and men in a country where about 70 percent are Roman catholic, in less than a year?
2. In Chechen, why would Russia fight these Moslem people after the old USSR just got out of Afghanistan where they lost thousands of troops again Moslem rebels?
3. In Bosnia-Herzegovina (formerly Yugoslavia), more than 200,000 people have been killed or are missing the ethno-religious warfare while millions have been driven from their homes since 1992. The Serbs reacted against a Muslim-Croat vote for independence, but why did it take so many lives before peace was negotiated with former President Jimmy Carter in late 1994?

4. In Panama, where thousands of Cuban refugees who just escaped from their island prison, why would Cubans riot against American troops who were there to help resettle them?
5. In Palestine, with the first agreement signed between Israel and the Palestinians, why are the Israelis allowing continued construction and settlement by the Jews in Efrat when this is against the agreement between these peoples so it threatens future peace talks?
6. In Brazil, why has the problem of hyperinflation and social inequalities been so long neglected?
7. In Thailand, where children are involved in prostitution and AIDS is spreading, why isn't the government doing more to stop these crimes against children? AIDS cases in Asia has grown from 30,000 to 360,000 with some of it out of the commercial sex trade where children are involved. Since the discovery of AIDS in the early 1980's, over 243,423 people have died nationwide in America. Research in the U.S.A. has found that women diagnosed with AIDS virus tend to die faster than men. No mental reason was found but a theory exists that women may wait longer before they seek treatment. [(1994), December 28). AIDS study finds disparity in death rates. *Kansas City Star,* page A-4].
8. In Cyprus, why is the conflict between Greece and Turkey not solved after all these years?

Appendix O

౸ᙣ

It's a Small World Worth Improving

How often we have heard the words from "It's a Small World" to "He's Got the Whole World In His Hands." These words illustrate how persons find each other in a global village of billions of people, and a tiny planet in a huge universe created by a first cause some call God. The 1994 Cairo, Egypt United Nations International Conference on Population and Development dealt with a plan to stabilize world population at under 7.8 billion by the year 2050 illustrated conflicts and controversy on how this will ever be done.

Organizations like the International Association of Educators for World Peace, related as a non-governmental organization of the United nations, have, since 1970, done a great deal through conferences, publications and contacts with world leaders to educate persons about present conflicts and stop wars throughout the world. The point is that as some of us travel around the world we meet former friends and acquaintances in foreign nations far from our homes, or these former friends and acquaintances from other countries come to see us after many years of separation. It is remarkable the insights of these reunions by plan or by coincidence. We learn how these nations have achieved some success and faced the serious stress of world conditions. Having had many of these experiences with persons from other lands, it is always a joyous and genuine event to see those who we have known over the years and to share what we have learned since our last meeting. By studying the goals and greatness of other nations, we discover how far America has to improve.

Dobyns and Crawford-Mason, (1994), criticize the problems and the shortcomings of America to keep us realistic and humble compared to other nations as follows:

According to a *New York Times* survey reported on December 29, 1994, a majority of Japanese polled believe the U.S.A. will continue to be the number one world economic power while a majority of Americans polled believe Japan will continue to be the second greatest economic world power.

> Americans are being beaten in international trade, we are losing wealth, and we are beginning to run out of national resources. We don't adequately educate our youth, we have more people locked up than any nation on earth, and American's suffer more crimes of violence than any other people. We Americans have created what may be the world's finest health care system, but it's too expensive for some of us to use. (Dobyns, L. and Crawford-Mason, C. (1994). *Thinking about quality: Progress, wisdom and the Deming philosophy.* New York, New York. Random House, page 241).

Winston Churchill, the former World War II Prime Minster of England, whose mother was an American, once said: "You can always count on the Americans to do the right thing—after they've tried everything else."

Appendix P

ℰℭℜ

What Can We Learn From Disasters?

In life, it is important what we can learn from disasters for it is certain one or many will beset us in life. Here are some lessons from higher education related personnel:

1. Charles Pell, former head football coach at the University of Florida in Gainsville, Florida, suffered many personal setbacks and unknown to him had a lifelong severe case of depression, so he tried to commit suicide but fortunately failed. He received excellent mental health treatment and support from his family and friends. Today, he has a job in business and is helping depressed persons from the U.S. and Cuba find a new life like he discovered.
2. Harold Kushner—Rabbit Temple Israel of Natick, Massachusetts—lost his 14 year old son to a rare disease. Out of his tragedy, he wrote a book that has helped many people globally entitled, *When Bad Things Happen to Good People*.
3. Helen Keller, born blind, deaf and dumb in the USA, through a genius teacher, Anne Sullivan, she learned to read, write

and speak before audiences from colleges to civic groups worldwide.

4. Wilma Rudolph, famous Olympic athlete, was as a young girl, handicapped with leg problems. Yet, she kept exercising her legs and developed into a great runner and famous 1960 sprinter and three-time gold medal winner.

5. B.G.E.—mother, homemaker, school teacher, business woman, and volunteer leader—has faced, with a faith and sense of humor, many difficulties in life such as overcoming a Northwestern University travel seminar to European countries; hosting foreign students in her home; loss of teenage son and husband; two hip replacements; near head-on automobile accidents; many hospitalizations due to illnesses; several falls down stairs; job loss due to gender discrimination; disease epidemics from polio to flu; arthritis; making a hundred-year-old run down house into a lovely home; keeping a garden going for 80 years; and surviving below zero icy winters for 90 years.

6. Frank Charles Laubach, founder of the "Each One Teach One" literacy teaching method, was the author of over forty books as he traveled to one hundred and three countries developing literacy primers in three hundred and twelve languages. Laubach was a model missionary and adult educator. [Lawson, J. G. (1989). *A historical study of the impact of the Christian development on the contribution of Frank C. Laubach in literacy education.* Denton, Texas: Unpublished doctoral dissertation in the Department of Higher and Adult Education at the University of North Texas]. Some of the crisis events he overcame were:

a) A graduate education in conflict with his personal basic faith belief system;

b) In Mindanao, Philippines he faced many physical, emotional and spiritual challenges of life and death conditions;

c) He and his wife lost three children who died in their infancy in the Philippines while a fourth child had to go with his wife to the U.S.A. to recover from a serious case of boils that often precedes malaria;

d) He suffered from flu, appendicitis, para-typhoid, a strained leg muscle and an ulcerated eye that made him a semi-invalid for two years in the Philippines; and

e) He died of acute leukemia at the age of 85, and he remained active until the final days of his life on March 28, 1973.

Appendix Q

ଯେଓଷ

Crisis Events In American Higher Education

S ome of the crisis situations in American higher education in 1995 are:

1. Many universities do not have enough qualified American graduate students in the physical and biological sciences and mathematics so the graduate assistantships are filled with foreign students, many from Asian nations such as China, India, Taiwan, and Korea. Some of these foreign students are over qualified students coming in as some are medical doctors to take a masters degree in physics or biology.
   Foreign professionals—about 65,000 annually—are working in America in areas where our citizens are in short supply such as computer programming, physical therapy, medicine, teaching (often higher education) and engineering field. These foreigners, however, do take jobs away from recent college graduates, minorities, women and immigrants. Sometimes, American businesses are dishonest as they hire these foreign specialists so to avoid paying these workers the prevailing wage, or when once hired, they reduce their pay to

increase their business profits. The foreign workers usually don't complain for fear of losing their jobs so the unfair labor conditions continue. As a result of the government allowing foreign workers, this removes incentives for businesses to train American or immigrants in these short supply specialized fields.

2. Thousands of foreign students are here as political refugees from their nations, and they will try to stay here to gain green card residence status and eventual naturalized citizenship while their native country will continue to suffer from a brain drain.

3. State legislatures and the federal government are providing less money for higher education proportionately to student number than in past years.

4. College graduates are not finding jobs suited to their education because of a shortage of jobs in America.

5. More American college graduates are seeking jobs overseas because they can't find suitable positions in their country.

6. Re-engineering, restructuring and reorganization approaches in American higher education are reducing faculties, staff and graduate assistantships due to a shortage of funding.

7. Federal financial aid programs continue to be taken advantage of by some post-secondary institutions as some administrators are doing criminal acts and thousands of students are irresponsible in paying back their loans. This immoral behavior has caused some congressmen to be against federal financial aide programs and to reduce these programs each year to college students. The 1995 Federal Congress is suggesting tax saving benefits for parents who send their children to college. However, experts predict state legislatures may be encouraged to raise tuition as much as the tax break would create. [Honan, W. H. *Minneapolis Star Journal*, page 4-A].

8. More foundations and businesses are favoring to help elementary and secondary schools with funding to draw more money away from higher education institutions' needs.

9. Only about 30 university athletic programs pay for themselves with the football programs the most costly. Some universities lose several millions of dollars each year on their football programs alone. At many universities, the highest paid staff are men football and basketball coaches with many bonuses and benefits totaling hundreds of thousands of dollars. Extra income comes from tennis shoe commissions to television program pay checks. Other problems with athletic programs

have been the criminal behavior of some athletes from raping to stealing to cheating and to drugging.

10. Grade inflation at some institutions of higher education may affect the quality of learning of students. This inflation may affect the motivation and skill level of students.

11. Alcohol, tobacco and illegal drug use continue to be problems among college students. The number of college students who abuse alcohol is alarming because of potential falls and driving accidents. About 3,000 teenagers per day start smoking with predictions that one-fourth of them die early from heart disease and lung cancer. Over 25,000 die annually from drunken driving with the majority youthful drivers from 14 to 24 years.

12. College students face other serious problems from an increasing number of HIV/AIDS and sexual disease victims to those committing suicide.

13. Millions of illegal immigrants are a problem in taking jobs away from legal immigrants and citizens in America.

Appendix R

ℬﻮᏆ

Case Study: Texas A & M University Leaders Admit Mistakes

On January 5, 1995 a report from the President of Texas A & M University admitted that there were many problems caused by personnel at this university. For example, here are some selective problems:

1. Some administrators of athletics' errors have caused the university to be put on NCAA probation;
2. Some administrators have allowed illegal activities on hiding the purchases of alcohol;
3. Some administrators overlooked research protocols, privately orchestrated multimillion dollar business deals and broke laws by awarding service contracts without competitive bidding;
4. Some administrators have ignored rules and regulations;
5. Some administrators failed to assess the wisdom of having a branch overseas campus in Japan so over $7 million dollars was lost before the branch was closed in 1994;
6. One administrator and his wife illegally solicited a free pleasure trip to New York City from a company that awarded a multimillion dollar contract to run the university bookstore.

Dr. Ray M. Bowen, first year President of Texas A & M, in response to these problems said: "We perceived ourselves to be unconstrained by rules and regulations. Our management has failed us. It has failed to exhibit the proper leadership; failed to accept responsibilities; failed to install a passion for institutional integrity on the part of all of our employees. It has something to apologize for because we are put in this position of public humiliation; because we violated policies and didn't honor the public trust as we should." [Associated Press Staff. (1995, January 7). Officials accept blame. *Denton Record-Chronicle,* page B-1 and B-2].

Appendix S

ဣၟလ

The Information Age and Its Importance

A 1994 economics book was published that stated that the chief resources are still only labor, land and capital, while ignoring information or knowledge as a key resource according to Dr. Newt Gingrich, former Speaker of the U.S. House of Representatives. The author has met three scholars that Dr. Gingrich mentions in his college courses. He has read some of their works and advocates studying their ideas.

Dr. Gingrich, one Professor of History of West Georgia College in Carrollton, Georgia, listed these scholars, Dr. Kenneth Boulding, Dr. Alvin Toffler and Dr. Peter Drucker, as having important ideas to study.

Alvin Toffler has written such books as *Future Shock, War and Anti-War in the 21st Century, The Adaptive Corporation, Power Shift, Third Wave and Creating a New Civilization: The Politics of the Third Wave.* He is a friend of Dr. Gingrich, however, they do not agree on all issues, but one they both emphasize is that information or knowledge is the key source we need to acknowledge as well as use wisely now.

Dr. Toffler has indicated that information or knowledge is the key and a good social thinker's characteristics should include, which come close to what an EDHE 6510 student studies:

1. knowledge of history;
2. knowledge of theories of sociology and psychology;
3. ability to think globally;
4. ability to think creatively;
5. ability to think futuristically;
6. ability to think family values;
7. ability to think civilization scales; and
8. ability to think U.S. Constitution issues.

In his American Civilization course at Reinhardt College, in Waleska, Georgia, Dr. Gingrich told his students several points such as: "I don't think you should trust anybody in power . . . Life is hard . . . Freedom is frustrating. You can shrink government without hurting people with special needs, and my model here is Franklin Delano Roosevelt, who by the way had a disability." [Associated Press Staff. (1995, January 8). Hometown folks welcome back Gingrich. *Denton Record-Chronicle,* page 9A].